Bron Johnson

THE
TRAEGER GRILL
BIBLE

Fish VS Meat

2 cookbooks in 1

The total wood pellet smoker cookbook with juicy recipes to turn
every beginner into the complete pitmaster

- THE -

EST. **OLD** 1999
TEXAS
PITMASTER

TRAVIS COUNTY

Recipes by Bron Johnson

Photography: Humbert Castillo

Graphic design: Tori Vergara

Editorial coordination: Joe Garcia and Humbert Castillo

First edition March 2021

TABLE OF CONTENTS

ABOUT BRON JOHNSON

Author of "The Traeger Grill Bible Series", Bron has spent most of his life smelling of wood-fired smoke. Bron wasn't always a professional pitmaster. He spent years as a commercial banker, and it was his bank that would eventually lead him to BBQ. The bank held a BBQ competition every year, and as an adamant griller, Bron felt he'd be able to hold his own. Once the competition started, he was in awe of the whole culture.

Teams smoking meat, drinking beer, and telling stories. Growing up in the South, he knew BBQ, but the culture around the competition added a whole new level of inspiration.

Before retiring in 1999, he served his Country in the Military. Bronson has two sons and two grandchildren. He lives in Austin, Texas, with his wife of 59 years. When not in the backyard smoking, roasting & grilling meats, he can be found tending his vegetable garden, fishing, or golfing. Peter and his wife enjoy traveling the Country in their RV - but he never leaves home without his tailgate portable wood pellet smoker-grill.

INTRODUCTION

A wood pellet grill uses proprietary wood pellets as fuel. This is different from a wood grill, and especially a charcoal grill.

Joe Traeger is the inventor of the wood pellet grill. He came up with the idea after he noticed his gas grill was in flames as he was preparing to cook for his family. That was in 1988. Today, pellet grills give consumers the flavor of wood smoke with the convenience of a gas grill.

Benefits of a Pellet Grill

We already know that pellet grills can be used to smoke, grill, bake and even braise food, and with all those capabilities it's no surprise that they act more like an outdoor oven than a traditional grill. The options for what to cook on a pellet grill are nearly endless because unlike other grills or smokers, a pellet grill allows you to cook something low and slow — or hotter and faster. You can also set a specific temperature which makes for consistent, efficient cooking every time. With no direct heat cooking and no open flame, you don't even have to worry about flare- ups!

Wood Pellet Grill vs. Gas Grill

The biggest difference between a pellet grill and a gas grill: the flavor! Pellet grills are powered by hardwood pellets and thus impart a naturally sweet, spicy, smoky flavor to everything you cook; a flavor that is unmatched by cooking on gas or charcoal grills. The team at Traeger says: *"The smoke acts as a wholly separate seasoning, adding a deeper and more robust flavor to whatever you decide to cook"*.

The flavor of cooking with wood pellets doesn't even compare to the flavor of cooking on a gas grill. Sure, you can argue that cooking over an open flame like you would on a gas grill gives off flavor, but what if you could get that meaty, smoky flavor without the inevitable ashy, burnt and blackened taste? That's where your pellet grill comes in. Heat is generated through combustion, by igniting wood pellets and circulating heat through a fan system. Much like a convection oven, this allows us to set and maintain a specific temperature
without worrying about the unpredictability of open fire flare-ups.

Wood Pellet Grill vs. Charcoal Grill

Although charcoal grills are certainly known for smoky flavor, there's one major difference that sets pellet grills apart from their charcoal counterpart: temperature regulation. Whatever temperature you decide to set your pellet grill to, you can be certain that it will maintain it. One of the biggest downfalls of a charcoal grill is that although it can achieve high temperatures, it's difficult to maintain high temperatures. We've all been there; you've heated your coals to the perfect temperature and before you know it, they're cooling off again! Pellet grills allow you to set a specific cooking temperature (some even support the use of an internal therm- ometer that pairs with your Bluetooth), so you can check on the doneness of your meat from the comfort of your couch. This system makes for a much more predictable, manageable and convenient grilling experience.

Overall, pellet grills are an exciting advancement in barbecuing. Most commonly known as "smokers," these grills are powered by hardwood pellets and act more like an outdoor oven than a standard gas or charcoal grill.

Wood pellet grills are one of the hottest trends in grilling right now. If you just got one or are about to, you've no doubt wondered how to use a wood pellet grill.

Wood pellet grills use real wood, all-natural wood pellets as fuel but also req uire an electrical outlet for power. Unlike propane, natural gas, or charcoal grills, burning pellets is not harmful to the environment. They come in a variety of flavors and are FDA approved.

Let's get started!

MEAT CUTS

PORK

Pork might not be my favorite meat, but it just might be my best. I have spent hours in front of my grill, prepping ribs and pork shoulders. As a frequent host of large parties, including a yearly rematch of Bad Santa with my hooligan high school friends, I had to start somewhere—and pork was a great place to start.

Pork has a salty flavor that cannot be mistaken. Though it can get in the way at times, the fat content in pork allows it to be both juicy and tender.

Pork goes exceptionally well with sweet flavors, and I refer to that a lot. Pick up some local honey; it supports the beekeepers, farmers, and markets in the area. Plus, local honey tastes better. Brown sugar is delicious with pork, too. And whenever I visit a buddy in Toronto, I always pick up some Canadian maple syrup in the duty-free shop on the way home to have on hand for pork recipes.

1.   Head
2.   Clear Plate
3.   Back Fat
4.   Boston Butt/Shoulder
5.   Loin/Tenderloin
6.   Ham
7.   Cheek
8.   Picnic Shoulder
9.   Ribs
10.   Bacon/Belly
11.   Hock

RIBS

Ribs, particularly baby back ribs, are my best dish. If there's one thing I do as well as James LeBron throws a basketball, it's smoking ribs. I will speak in general terms when dealing with pork ribs, spare ribs, and baby backs. You want to select a cut with a good amount of fat in both cases, but it should be consistent throughout. Too much fat, especially if it is only in certain places, can make for an unappetizingly fatty bite.

We will prep our ribs the way you see them at a competition, not at the local chain barbecue restaurant. These will have just the slightest pull. To them just before the meat slips and falls off the bone. If you want the meat slipping and sliding off the bone, cook them a little longer.

TIPS & TECHNIQUES

Remove the membrane. That weird membrane on the back of ribs (sometimes called silver skin) can make them harder to pull off the bone and less tender. To get pit master-level results each time, remove the membrane.

Use mustard as a binder. Mustard works excellent as a binder for your rub on fatty meats such as ribs. Rub plain yellow mustard or another smooth mustard over your ribs before or after your rub. This will keep your rub on your meat and not all over your drip pan. Use whatever liquid you like best (including beer or wine, but not liquor) for your spritz or your wrap. When watching a competition cook prep ribs with Mountain Dew, I asked why. "It's what my brother and I like and what we had, so we just started using it," he told me. I use Pepsi; my dad and brother use apple juice. Use what you like, or see what other pitmasters are using and try that for a change. It's a great place to experiment.

Sauce it—just don't overdo it. Again, saucing is a natural preference. At parties, I always have a plate of ribs with just a dry rub. Over the years, my ribs have gone from dry to heavily sauced, and now I just use a light sweet coating. As you will see in the recipes, we also have other ways to achieve sweetness.

Country-style ribs are ribs. Cook boneless country-style ribs the same way you would other ribs. The smoked flavor is excellent, and they are incredibly tender when done.

PORK SHOULDER

Pulled pork is something pit masters love. Not just because it's easy and good, but because it typically means leftovers for days. Sliders, nachos, and sandwiches are all day-two and day-three renditions of the pulled-pork-leftover week. A good-size pork shoulder could feed an army—or at least an army of kids just back from baseball, gymnastics, or soccer. When selecting your pork shoulder—also called pork

Butt or Boston butt—it doesn't matter if you choose one with or without a bone. However, do check the fat content. You want some fat, or your pork will dry out, but too much can be overly fatty, just like ribs. The fat cap should be less than 1 inch deep.

TIPS & TECHNIQUES

Inject your pork shoulder for extra moisture and flavor. Using tea, inject your shoulder. A good shoulder will have a nice flavorful bark, but injecting will give it flavor everywhere.

Smoke your pork longer for a good "bark." The bark isn't just on trees or what your dog does. The bark is that delicious crust on the outside of well-smoked meat. The bark develops when the meat and rub are combined with uninterrupted smoke for an extended time. A good pork shoulder will have a good, dark bark. To increase the amount of bark, smoke the pork longer, unwrapped.

Use your hands when pulling the meat— it's just easier. There are some new cool claws available that can be used for pulling pork. They keep your hands from getting hot and greasy. Fact is, though, with those, the pull never really feels right. I have a pair of gloves I wear under food service gloves. The gloves keep my hands from burning but let me pull the meat precisely as I like it.

TENDERLOINS

Pork tenderloins are among the simplest smoke pre- partitions on the grill, but they're always impressive. I smoke a couple of tenderloins for my family every couple of weeks, and they never get tired of them. The pellet grill or smoker does a fantastic job with tenderloins, ensuring a juicy result each time.

When selecting tenderloins, as with most pork, the key is fat content. I try to limit the fat content on my tenderloins. A pellet grill will work to keep them moist and will limit dried-out areas.

TIPS & TECHNIQUES

If you're lazy, just smoke them. The Smoke setting of the pellet grill works great to get your meat to

The temperature while always keeping it moist. Use a reverse sear. Searing is usually done first, before cooking the meat entirely. When we do it last, after fully smoking the meat, we call it a reverse sear.

If your grill has an open flame option, like a flame broiler, use that; otherwise, crank up your grill's temperature as high as it will go.

After smoking the tenderloins until their internal temperature reaches 135°F to 140°F, sear them off at a higher temperature until they reach 145°F, about 3 to 5 minutes per side. Pork tenderloins are a great candidate for marinating. Teriyaki-marinated pork tenderloin tastes fantastic, and the meat can take on the marinade flavor in as little as 30 minutes.

BEEF

When I think of smoking and barbecue, my mind immediately goes to beef: significant cuts of brisket and tri-tip, steaks over a flame. Fortunately, with today's grill technology, all of these are possible on a pellet grill. But the dream of so many pitmasters is that perfect Texas-style brisket. We have all spent hours researching how best to achieve it: Wrapped or unwrap- ped? Foil or butcher paper? How long should it take? We also want steaks that even the owner of the best steakhouse would pay for—the smoke and the butter and the fire, all infused with the smell of searing meat. That's what we aim for in our backyards.

This is why I think "beef" when I think of smoking and barbecue.

Selecting beef is made more accessible by its grade. We'll go into this here, as well as some other tips to make you a master of low-and-slow meat cooking.

1.	Neck
2.	Chuck
3.	Rib
4.	Short Loin
5.	Sirloin
6.	Tenderloin
7.	Top Sirloin

8.   Rump Cap
9.   Round
10.   Brisket
11.   Shoulder Clod
12.   Short Plate
13.   Flank

BRISKET

In my experience, brisket tends to be the gold standard and the most difficult to cook on the pellet grill. Many look at the perfect brisket with reverence and hope for the day when they'll successfully achieve it. Discussions fill message boards on the bend test, the pull test, and the like. The problem with this line of thinking around brisket? Well, it's actually not that difficult to make! Brisket, just like anything else, can be perfected with practice and patience.

When selecting the perfect brisket—and I am referring- ring to a whole brisket, with both the point and flat cuts (usually separated at most butchers) intact— the key is not too fat. If you buy a brisket with a huge fat cap, you are just going to cut it off. Also, I suggest spending the extra money on the highest grade of brisket available to you. A cheap brisket can equal a tough brisket. Brisket is not a cheap cut anyway, so spend the money for the best cut.

TIPS & TECHNIQUES

Get rid of that fat cap. A large fat cap is just not appetizing if you leave it on when you smoke your brisket. Use a boning knife or whatever knife you have available and cut the fat cap down to about ¼ inch. Trimming the fat cap will decrease the fattiness of your brisket, but leaving it partially there will keep the meat moist.

Wrap, don't wrap. You choose. Both aluminum foil and butcher paper can be used for wrapping—again, it is all about preference. However, the one thing I will say about wrapping is don't do it until after the stall, 165°F to 170°F. Wrapping too early cuts down on your bark development, and your brisket won't be as smoky.

If you don't wrap the meat, spritz it or use a water pan. Spritzing with liquid, like apple juice or plain water, will ensure your brisket stays moist. A water pan can be used in a pellet grill just like you would in any other type of grill, but be careful not to spill it. Simply fill a metal pan with water and place it inside the grill. Have a flat drain pan; the water pan will sit.

Let's Get Cooking!

FINEST FISH & SEAFOOD RECIPES

Salmon BBQ with Togarashi

Preparation Time: 5 Minutes

Cooking Time: 20 Minutes

Servings: 3

Ingredients:

- One salmon fillet

- 1/4 cup olive oil

- 1/2 tbsp kosher salt

- 1 tbsp Togarashi seasoning

Directions:

1.   Preheat your Wood Pellet Grill to 4000 F.

2.   Place the salmon on a sheet lined with non-stick foil with the skin side down.

3.   Rub the oil into the meat, then sprinkle salt and Togarashi.

4.   Place the salmon on the grill and cook for 20 minutes or until the internal temperature reaches 1450 F with the lid closed.

5.   Remove from the Traeger and serve when hot.

Grilled Rockfish

Preparation Time: 10 Minutes

Cooking Time: 20 Minutes

Servings: 6

Ingredients:

- Six rockfish fillets

- One lemon, sliced

- 3/4 tbsp salt

- 2 tbsp fresh dill, chopped

- 1/2 tbsp garlic powder

- 1/2 tbsp onion powder

- 6 tbsp butter

Directions:

1. Preheat your Wood Pellet Grill to 4000 F.

2. Season the fish with salt, dill, garlic, and onion powder on both sides, then place it in a baking dish.

3. Place a pat of butter and a lemon slice on each fillet. Place the baking dish in the Traeger and close the lid.

4. Cook for 20 minutes or until the fish is no longer translucent and is flaky.

5. Remove from Traeger and let rest before serving.

Delicious Grilled Lingcod

Preparation Time: 10 Minutes

Cooking Time: 15 Minutes

Servings: 6

Ingredients:

- 2 lb. lingcod fillets

- 1/2 tbsp salt

- 1/2 tbsp white pepper

- 1/4 tbsp cayenne pepper

- Lemon wedges

Directions:

1. Preheat your Wood Pellet Grill to 3750 F.

2. Place the lingcod on a parchment paper or a grill mat

3. Season the fish with salt, pepper, and top with lemon wedges.

4. Cook the fish for 15 minutes or until the internal temperature reaches 1450 F.

Crab Stuffed Lingcod

Preparation Time: 20 Minutes

Cooking Time: 30 Minutes

Servings: 6

Ingredients:

Lemon cream sauce

- Four garlic cloves

- One shallot

- One leek

- 2 tbsp olive oil

- 1 tbsp salt

- 1/4 tbsp black pepper

- 3 tbsp butter

- 1/4 cup white wine

- 1 cup whipping cream

- 2 tbsp lemon juice

- 1 tbsp lemon zest

Crab mix

- 1 lb. crab meat

- 1/3 cup mayo

- 1/3 cup sour cream

- 1/3 cup lemon cream sauce

- 1/4 green onion, chopped

- 1/4 tbsp black pepper

- 1/2 tbsp old bay seasoning

Fish

- 2 lb. lingcod

- 1 tbsp olive oil

- 1 tbsp salt

- 1 tbsp paprika

- 1 tbsp green onion, chopped

- 1 tbsp Italian parsley

Directions:

Lemon cream sauce

1.   Chop garlic, shallot, and leeks, then add to a saucepan with oil, salt, pepper, and butter.

2.   Sauté over medium heat until the shallot is translucent.

3.   Deglaze with white wine, then add whipping cream. Bring the sauce to boil, reduce heat, and simmer for 3 minutes.

4.   Remove from heat and add lemon juice and lemon zest. Transfer the sauce to a blender and blend until smooth.

5.   Set aside 1/3 cup for the crab mix

Crab mix

1.   Add all the fixings to a mixing bowl and mix thoroughly until well combined.

2.   Set aside

Fish

1.   Fire up your Wood Pellet Grill to high heat, then slice the fish into 6- ounce portions.

2.   Lay the fish on its side on a cutting board and slice it 3/4 way through the middle leaving a 1/2 inch on each end to have a nice pouch.

3.   Rub the oil into the fish, then place them on a baking sheet. Sprinkle with salt.

4.   Stuff crab mix into each fish, then sprinkle paprika and place it on the grill.

5.   Cook for 15 minutes or more if the fillets are more than 2 inches thick.

6.   Remove the fish and transfer to serving platters. Pour the remaining lemon cream sauce on each fish and garnish with onions and parsley.

Smoked Shrimp

Preparation Time: 10 Minutes

Cooking Time: 10 Minutes

Servings: 6

Ingredients:

- 1 lb. tail-on shrimp, uncooked

- 1/2 tbsp onion powder

- 1/2 tbsp garlic powder

- 1/2 tbsp salt

- 4 tbsp teriyaki sauce

- 2 tbsp green onion, minced

- 4 tbsp sriracha mayo

Directions:

1. Peel the shrimp shells leaving the tail on, then wash well and rise.

2. Drain well and pat dry with a paper towel.

3. Preheat your Wood Pellet Grill to 4500 F.

4. Season the shrimp with onion powder, garlic powder, and salt. Place the shrimp in the Traeger and cook for 6 minutes on each side.

5. Remove the shrimp from the Traeger and toss with teriyaki sauce, then garnish with onions and mayo.

Grilled Shrimp Kabobs

Preparation Time: 5 Minutes

Cooking Time: 10 Minutes

Servings: 4

Ingredients:

- 1 lb. colossal shrimp, peeled and deveined

- 2 tbsp. oil

- 1/2 tbsp. garlic salt

- 1/2 tbsp. salt

- 1/8 tbsp. pepper

- Six skewers

Directions:

1. Preheat your Wood Pellet Grill to 3750 F.

2. Pat the shrimp dry with a paper towel.

3. In a mixing bowl, mix oil, garlic salt, salt, and pepper

4. Toss the shrimp in the mixture until well coated.

5. Skewer the shrimps and cook in the Traeger with the lid closed for 4 minutes.

6. Open the lid, flip the skewers, cook for another 4 minutes, or wait until the shrimp is pink and the flesh is opaque.

7. Serve.

Bacon-Wrapped Shrimp

Preparation Time: 20 Minutes

Cooking Time: 10 Minutes

Servings: 12

Ingredients:

- 1 lb. raw shrimp

- 1/2 tbsp salt

- 1/4 tbsp garlic powder

- 1 lb. bacon, cut into halves

Directions:

1. Preheat your Wood Pellet Grill to 3500 F.

2. Remove the shells and tails from the shrimp, then pat them dry with the paper towels.

3. Sprinkle salt and garlic on the shrimp, then wrap with bacon and secure with a toothpick.

4. Place the shrimps on a baking rack greased with cooking spray.

5. Cook for 10 minutes, flip and cook for another 10 minutes, or until the bacon is crisp enough.

6. Remove from the Traeger and serve.

Spot Prawn Skewers

Preparation Time: 10 Minutes

Cooking Time: 10 Minutes

Servings: 6

Ingredients:

- 2 lb. spot prawns

- 2 tbsp oil

- Salt and pepper to taste

Directions:

1.   Preheat your Wood Pellet Grill to 4000 F.

2.   Skewer your prawns with soaked skewers, then generously sprinkle with oil, salt, and pepper.

3.   Place the skewers on the grill, then cook with the lid closed for 5 minutes on each side.

4.   Remove the skewers and serve when hot.

Bacon-wrapped Scallops

Preparation Time: 15 Minutes

Cooking Time: 20 Minutes

Servings: 8

Ingredients:

- 1 lb. sea scallops

- 1/2 lb. bacon

- Sea salt

Directions:

1.   Preheat your Wood Pellet Grill to 3750 F.

2.   Pat dry the scallops with a towel, then wrap them with a piece of bacon and secure with a toothpick.

3.   Lay the scallops on the grill with the bacon side down. Close the lid and cook for 5 minutes on each side.

4.   Keep the scallops on the bacon side so that you will not get grill marks on the scallops.

5.   Serve and enjoy.

Lobster Tail

Preparation Time: 10 Minutes

Cooking Time: 15 Minutes

Servings: 2

Ingredients:

- 10 oz lobster tail

- 1/4 tbsp old bay seasoning

- 1/4 tbsp Himalayan salt

- 2 tbsp butter, melted

- 1 tbsp fresh parsley, chopped

Directions:

1. Preheat your Wood Pellet Grill to 4500 F.

2. Slice the tail down the middle, then season it with bay seasoning and salt.

3. Place the tails directly on the grill with the meat side down. Grill for 15 minutes or until the internal temperature reaches 1400 F.

4. Remove from the Traeger and drizzle with butter.

5. Serve when hot garnished with parsley.

Roasted Honey Salmon

Preparation Time: 5 Minutes

Cooking Time: 1 Hour

Servings: 4

Ingredients:

- Two cloves garlic, grated

- Two tablespoon ginger, minced

- One teaspoon honey

- One teaspoon sesame oil

- Two tablespoon lemon juice

- 1 teaspoon chili paste

- Four salmon fillets

- Two tablespoon soy sauce

Directions:

1. Set your Wood Pellet Grill to smoke while the lid is open.

2. Do this for 5 minutes.

3. Preheat your wood pellet grill to 400 degrees F.

4. Combine all the ingredients except salmon in a sealable plastic bag.

5. Shake to mix the ingredients.

6. Add the salmon.

7. Marinate inside the refrigerator for 30 minutes.

8.   Add the salmon to a roasting pan and place it on top of the grill.

9.   Close the lid and cook for 3 minutes.

10.   Flip the salmon and cook for another 3 minutes.

Blackened Salmon

Preparation Time: 10 Minutes

Cooking Time: 20 Minutes

Servings: 4

Ingredients:

- 2 lb. salmon, fillet, scaled and deboned

- 2 tablespoons olive oil

- Four tablespoons sweet dry rub

- One tablespoon cayenne pepper

- Two cloves garlic, minced

Directions:

1. Turn on your Wood Pellet Grill.

2. Set it to 350 degrees F.

3. Brush the salmon with the olive oil.

4. Sprinkle it with the dry rub, cayenne pepper, and garlic.

5. Grill for 5 minutes per side.

Grilled Cajun Shrimp

Preparation Time: 5 Minutes

Cooking Time: 25 Minutes

Servings: 8

Ingredients:

Dip

- 1/2 cup mayonnaise

- One teaspoon lemon juice

- 1 cup sour cream

- 1 clove garlic, grated

- 1 tablespoon Cajun seasoning

- One tablespoon hickory bacon rub

- One tablespoon hot sauce

- Chopped scallions

Shrimp

- 1/2 lb. shrimp, peeled and deveined

- Two tablespoons olive oil

- 1/2 tablespoon hickory bacon seasoning

- One tablespoon Cajun seasoning

Directions:

1.	Turn on your Wood Pellet Grill.

2.	Set it to 350 degrees F.

3.   Mix the dip ingredients in a bowl.

4.   Transfer to a small pan.

5.   Cover with foil.

6.   Place on top of the grill.

7.   Cook for 10 minutes.

8.   Coat the shrimp with the olive oil and sprinkle with the seasonings.

9.   Grill for 5 minutes per side.

10.   Pour the dip on top or serve with the shrimp.

Salmon Cakes

Preparation Time: 5 Minutes

Cooking Time: 25 Minutes

Servings: 4

Ingredients:

- 1 cup cooked salmon, flaked

- 1/2 red bell pepper, chopped

- Two eggs, beaten

- 1/4 cup mayonnaise

- 1/2 tablespoon dry sweet rub

- 1 1/2 cups breadcrumbs

- One tablespoon mustard

Directions:

1. Combine all the fixings except the olive oil in a bowl.

2. Form patties from this mixture.

3. Let sit for 15 minutes.

4. Turn on your Wood Pellet Grill.

5. Set it to 350 degrees F.

6. Add a baking pan to the grill.

7. Drizzle a little olive oil on top of the pan.

8. Add the salmon cakes to the pan.

9. Grill each side for 3 to 4 minutes.

Swordfish Steaks with Corn Salsa

Preparation Time: 10 Minutes

Cooking Time: 30 Minutes

Servings: 4

Ingredients:

- Four whole ears corn, husked

- Olive oil, as needed

- Salt and black pepper, to taste

- 1-pint cherry tomatoes

- One whole serrano chile, chopped

- One whole red onion, diced

- One whole lime, juiced

- Four whole swordfish fillets

Directions:

1.   When ready to cook, put the wood pellet grill to High and preheat for 15 minutes.

2.   Brush the corn with the olive oil and season with salt and pepper. Place the corn on the grill grate and grill for 12 to 15 minutes, or until cooked through and lightly browned. Set aside to cool.

3.   Once the corn has cooled, cut the kernels from the corn and transfer to a medium bowl. Stir in the tomatoes, serrano, red onion, and lime juice.

4.   Brush the swordfish fillets with the olive oil and season with salt and pepper.

5.	Arrange the fillets on the grill grate and grill for about 18 minutes, or until the fish is opaque and flakes easily when pressed with a fork.

6.	Serve the grilled swordfish topped with the corn salsa.

Grilled Oysters with Veggie Sauce

Preparation Time: 20 Minutes

Cooking Time: 25 Minutes

Servings: 4

Ingredients:

- Five tablespoons extra-virgin olive oil

- Two medium onions, chopped

- One medium red bell pepper, chopped

- Two lemons, juiced

- Three dried bay leaves

- Five tablespoons minced garlic

- Three tablespoons Traeger Chicken Rub

- Three teaspoons dried thyme

- ¼ cup white wine

- Five tablespoons hot pepper sauce

- Three tablespoons Worcestershire Sauce

- Four butter sticks

- 12 whole oysters, cleaned and shucked

- Italian cheese blend, as needed

Directions:

1.   When ready to cook, put the wood pellet grill to High and preheat, lid closed for 15 minutes.

2.   Heat the olive oil in a cast-iron pan over medium heat. Add the onions, bell peppers, lemon juice, bay leaves, garlic, Traeger Chicken Rub, and thyme to the pan. Sauté the vegetable mixture for 5 to 7 minutes, or until the onions are translucent and peppers are tender.

3.   Add the white wine, hot pepper sauce, Worcestershire Sauce, and butter to the pan. Sauté for another 15 minutes.

4.   Place the oysters and top with the sauce—Cook for 5 minutes.

5.   Top with Italian cheese and serve hot.

Crispy Fried Halibut Fish Sticks

Preparation Time: 10 Minutes

Cooking Time: 3 to 4 Minutes

Servings: 4

Ingredients:

- Extra-virgin olive oil, as needed

- 1½ pounds (680 g) halibut, rinsed, patted dry, and cut into 1-inch strips

- ½ cup all-purpose flour

- 1½ teaspoons salt

- One teaspoon ground black pepper

- Two large eggs

- 1½ cups panko bread crumbs

- Two tablespoons dried parsley

- One teaspoon dried dill weed

Directions:

1.   When ready to cook, put wood pellet grill temperature to 500°F (260°C) and preheat, lid closed for 15 minutes.

2.   Place a Dutch oven inside the grill to preheat for about 10 minutes, with enough olive oil to fry the fish.

3.   In a bowl, stir together the all-purpose flour, salt, and pepper. In a separate bowl, beat the eggs. In a third bowl, combine the panko, parsley, and dill.

4.   Dredge the fish fillets in the flour mixture, then the eggs and then the panko mixture.

5.   Place the coated fish fillets in the oil and fry for about 3 to 4 minutes, or until they reach an internal temperature of 130°F (54°C).

6.   Serve warm.

White Fish Steaks with Orange Basil Pesto

Preparation Time: 10 Minutes

Cooking Time: 15 Minutes

Servings: 4

Ingredients:

- 1 orange, juiced

- 2 cups fresh basil

- 1 cup chopped flat-leaf parsley

- ½ cup toasted walnuts

- 2 teaspoons orange zest

- ½ cup olive oil

- 1 cup grated Parmesan cheese

- 4 white fish steaks, rinsed and patted dry

- ½ teaspoon coarse sea salt

- ½ teaspoon black pepper

Directions:

1.   Make the pesto: In a food processor, combine the orange juice, basil, parsley, walnuts and orange zest and pulse until finely chopped. With the machine running, slowly drizzle in the olive oil until the mixture is emulsified.

2.   Scrape the pesto into a bowl and stir in the Parmesan cheese.

3.   Brush the fish steaks with olive oil on both sides and season with salt and pepper.

4.   Arrange the fish steaks on the grill grate. Grill for 12 to 15 minutes, turning once with a thin-bladed metal spatula, or until the fish is opaque and breaks into chunks when pressed with a fork.

5.   Transfer the steaks to a platter. Drizzle with the prepared pesto and serve immediately.

Lemony Salmon Fillets

Preparation Time: 10 Minutes

Cooking Time: 20 Minutes

Servings: 2

Ingredients:

- 2 tablespoons butter, softened

- 2 teaspoons fresh chopped dill, plus more for garnish

- 1 teaspoon lemon juice

- ½ teaspoon lemon zest

- ½ teaspoon salt

- Black pepper, to taste

- 4 (8-ounce / 227-g) salmon fillets, skin on

- 1 lemon, thinly sliced

Directions:

1. When fit to cook, set wood pellet grill temperature to 350°F (177°C) and preheat for 15 minutes.

2. Meanwhile, stir together all the ingredients, except for the salmon and lemon, in a bowl.

3. Generously spread the lemon-dill butter over the top of the salmon fillets and top with a slice of lemon.

4. Place the salmon fillets on the grill grate, skin-side facing down. Cook for 15 to 20 minutes, for a medium-rare salmon, or until the salmon is done to your liking.

5. Serve garnished with the fresh dill.

Grilled Salmon with Teriyaki Sauce

Preparation Time: 10 Minutes

Cooking Time: 15 Minutes

Servings: 2

Ingredients:

- 1 cup soy sauce

- 6 tablespoons brown sugar

- 1 tablespoon minced ginger

- 4 cloves garlic

- Juice and zest of 2 whole oranges

- 4 (6-ounce / 170-g) pieces salmon fillets

- 1 tablespoon sesame seeds

- Chopped scallions, as needed

Directions:

1.   In a saucepan, place the soy sauce, brown sugar, ginger, garlic, orange juice and zest. Bring to a boil and slowly boil for 1o minutes, or until a syrupy consistency is achieved, about a 50 percent reduction. Let cool completely. Add the salmon and sesame seeds and marinate for 1 hour.

2.   Remove the salmon from the marinade and bring the sauce to a boil.

3.   Place the salmon fillets straight on the grill grate, skin-side up. Cook for about 3 to 5 minutes per side. Until they are done until your liking and occasionally, brush the salmon with the sauce.

4.   Remove the salmon from the grill and serve topped with the toasted sesame seeds and chopped scallions.

BBQ Rainbow Trout

Preparation Time: 10 Minutes

Cooking Time: 15 Minutes

Servings: 1

Ingredients:

- 4 tablespoons butter

- Lemon juice, as needed

- 1 whole rainbow trout, rinsed

- 1 tablespoon salt

- 1 teaspoon chipotle pepper

- 2 whole oranges, sliced

- 4 sprigs thyme sprigs

- 3 whole bay leaves

- 1 clove garlic, chopped

Directions:

1.   When ready to cook, custom wood pellet grill temperature to 400°F (204°C) and preheat, lid closed for 15 minutes.

2.   Melt the butter in a pot over medium high heat. After the butter melts completely, it will begin to foam and the milk solids will begin to brown. After all foam subsides and the butter looks golden brown, remove the pan from the heat and drizzle in a bit of lemon juice to stop the browning process. Set aside.

3.   Layout a piece of foil 3 inches longer on each end than the fish. Drizzle the fish's exterior and cavity with the brown butter and

season with salt and chipotle powder. Stuff the cavity with the remaining ingredients and fold the foil into a packet.

4.   Place the packet directly on the grill grate and cook for about 15 minutes, or until the internal temperature has reached 145°F (63°C).

5.   Remove from the grill and serve hot.

Crab Legs

Preparation Time: 10 Minutes

Cooking Time: 30 Minutes

Servings: 4

Ingredients:

- 3 pounds (1.4 kg) crab legs, thawed and halved

- 1 cup butter, melted

- 2 tablespoons fresh lemon juice

- 2 cloves garlic, minced

- 1 tablespoon Traeger Fin & Feather Rub

Directions:

1. When ready to cook, custom wood pellet grill temperature to 350°F (177°C) and preheat, lid closed for 15 minutes.

2. Split the crab shells open lengthwise. Transfer to the roasting pan.

3. In a small bowl, stick together the butter, lemon juice, and garlic.

4. Spread the butter mixture over the crab legs, turning the legs to coat. Sprinkle the Traeger Fin & Feather Rub over the legs.

5. Place the pan on the grill grate. Cook for 20 to 30 minutes, or until warmed through, basting once or twice with the butter sauce from the pan's bottom.

6. Transfer the crab legs to a large platter and divide the sauce and accumulated juices between 4 dipping bowls. Serve topped with the parsley.

Grilled Buttery BBQ Oysters

Preparation Time: 10 Minutes

Cooking Time: 6 Minutes

Servings: 4

Ingredients:

- 1 pound (454 g) unsalted butter, softened

- 1 bunch green onions, chopped, plus more for garnish

- 2 cloves garlic, minced

- 1 tablespoon Meat Church Holy Gospel BBQ Rub

- 12 oysters, shucked, juice reserved

- ¼ cup seasoned bread crumbs

- 8 ounces (227 g) shredded Pepper Jack cheese

- Sweet & Heat BBQ Sauce, as needed

Directions:

1. Make the compound butter: Stir together the butter, green onions, garlic and Meat Church Holy Gospel BBQ Rub in a medium bowl.

2. Lay the butter on parchment paper. Roll it up to form a log and tie each end with cooking twine. Place in the freezer for an hour to solidify.

3. Sprinkle the bread crumbs over the oysters and place directly on the grill. Cook for 5 minutes, or until the edge of the oyster starts to curl slightly.

4.	After 5 minutes, place a spoonful of compound butter in the oysters. After the butter melts, add a pinch of Pepper Jack cheese. Cook for 1 more minute.

5.	Remove the oysters from the grill. Top the oysters with a squirt of Sweet & Heat BBQ Sauce and a few chopped onions. Let cool for 5 minutes before serving.

Smoked Vodka Salmon

Preparation Time: 5 Minutes

Cooking Time: 1 Hour

Servings: 4

Ingredients:

- 1 cup brown sugar

- 1 cup vodka

- ½ cup coarse salt

- 1 tablespoon black pepper

- 1 wild-caught salmon (1½ to 2 pounds / 680 to 907 g)

- 1 lemon, wedged, for serving

- Capers, for serving

Directions:

1.   In a small bowl, whisk together the brown sugar, vodka, salt, and pepper.

2.   Place the salmon in a large resealable bag. Pour in the marinade and massage into the salmon. Refrigerate for 2 to 4 hours.

3.   Remove, the salmon from the bag, rinse and pat dry with paper towels.

4.   Set wood pellet grill temperature to 180°F (82°C) and preheat, lid closed for 15 minutes.

5.   Place the salmon on the grill, skin-side down, and smoke for 30 minutes.

6.   Increase the temperature to 225°F (107°C) and continue to cook the salmon for an additional 45 to 60 minutes, or until the fish flakes easily when pressed with a fork.

7.   Serve with the lemons and capers.

Jerk Shrimp

Preparation Time: 15 Minutes

Cooking Time: 6 Minutes

Servings: 12

Ingredients:

- 2 pounds shrimp, peeled, deveined

- 3 tablespoons olive oil

For the Spice Mix:

- 1 teaspoon garlic powder

- 1 teaspoon of sea salt

- 1/4 teaspoon ground cayenne

- 1 tablespoon brown sugar

- 1/8 teaspoon smoked paprika

- 1 tablespoon smoked paprika

- 1/4 teaspoon ground thyme

- 1 lime, zested

Directions:

1.   Switch on the wood pellet grill, occupy the grill hopper with flavored wood pellets, power the grill onion the Traeger grill, close the grill hopper with flavored wood pellets, power the grill on by the control panel, select 'smoke' on the temperature set the temperature to 450 degrees F and let it heat for at least 5 minutes.

2.   Meanwhile, prepare the spice mix and for this, take a small dish, place all of its ingredients in it and stir until mixed.

3.	Take a large bowl, place shrimps in it, sprinkle with prepared spice mix, drizzle with oil and toss until well coated.

4.	When the grill has preheated, open the lid, place shrimps on the grill grate, close the grill and smoke for 3 minutes per side until firm and thoroughly cooked.

5.	When done, transfer shrimps to a dish and then serve.

Spicy Shrimp Skewers

Preparation Time: 10 Minutes

Cooking Time: 6 Minutes

Servings: 4

Ingredients:

- 2 pounds shrimp, peeled, and deveined

For the Marinade:

- 6 ounces Thai chilies

- 6 cloves of garlic, peeled

- 1 ½ teaspoon sugar

- 2 tablespoons Napa Valley rub

- 1 ½ tablespoon white vinegar

- 3 tablespoons olive oil

Directions:

1. Prepare the marinade and for this, place all of its ingredients in a food processor and then pulse for 1 minute until smooth.

2. Take a large bowl, place shrimps on it, add prepared marinade, toss until well coated, and let marinate for a minimum of 30 minutes in the refrigerator.

3. When ready to cook, switch on the wood pellet grill.

4. Fill the grill hopper with apple-flavored wood pellets.

5. Turn on the grill choose 'smoke' on the temperature dial, or set the temperature to 450 degrees F.

6. Let it preheat for a margin of 5 minutes.

7.   Meanwhile, remove shrimps from the marinade and then thread onto skewers.

8.   When the grill has preheated, open the lid, place shrimps' skewers on the grill grate, shut the grill and smoke for 3 minutes per side until firm.

9.   When done, transfer shrimps' skewers to a dish and then serve.

Lemon Garlic Scallops

Preparation Time: 10 Minutes

Cooking Time: 5 Minutes

Servings: 6

Ingredients:

- 1 dozen scallops

- 2 tablespoons chopped parsley

- Salt as needed

- 1 tablespoon olive oil

- 1 tablespoon butter, unsalted

- 1 teaspoon lemon zest

For the Garlic Butter:

- ½ teaspoon minced garlic

- 1 lemon, juiced

- 4 tablespoons butter, unsalted, melted

Directions:

1.	Switch on the wood pellet grill, fill the grill hopper with alder flavored wood pellets, power the grill on by using the control panel, choose 'smoke' on the temperature dial, or set the temperature 400 degrees F and let it preheat for a minimum of 15 minutes.

2.	Meanwhile, remove frill from scallops, pat dry with paper towels and then season with salt and black pepper.

3.   When the grill has preheated, open the lid, place a skillet on the grill grate, add butter and oil, and when the butter melts, place seasoned scallops on it and then cook for 2 minutes until seared.

4.   Meanwhile, prepare the garlic butter and for this, take a small bowl, place all of its ingredients in it and then whisk until combined.

5.   Flip the scallops, top with some of the prepared garlic butter, and cook for another minute.

6.   When done, transfer scallops to a dish, top with remaining garlic butter, sprinkle with parsley and lemon zest, and then serve.

Halibut in Parchment

Preparation Time: 15 Minutes

Cooking Time: 15 Minutes

Servings: 4

Ingredients:

- 16 asparagus spears, trimmed, sliced into 1/2-inch pieces

- 2 ears of corn kernels

- 4 ounces halibut fillets, pin bones removed

- 2 lemons, cut into 12 slices

- Salt as needed

- Ground black pepper as needed

- 2 tablespoons olive oil

- 2 tablespoons chopped parsley

Directions:

1. Turn on the wood pellet grill, power the grill on by using the control panel, key 'smoke' on the temperature dial, or set the temperature to 450 degrees F and let it preheat for a minimal of 5 minutes.

2. Meanwhile, cut out 18-inch long parchment paper, place a fillet in the center of each parchment, season with salt and black pepper, and then drizzle with oil.

3. Cover each fillet with three lemon slices, overlapping slightly, sprinkle one-fourth of asparagus and corn on each fillet, season with some salt and black pepper, and seal the fillets and vegetables tightly to prevent steam from escaping the packet.

---

4.   When the grill has preheated, open the lid, place fillet packets on the grill grate, shut the grill and smoke for 15 minutes until packets have turned slightly brown and puffed up.

5.   When done, transfer packets to a dish, let them stand for 5 minutes, then cut 'X' in the center of each packet, carefully uncover the fillets a vegetable, sprinkle with parsley, and then serve.

Chilean Sea Bass

Preparation Time: 30 Minutes

Cooking Time: 40 Minutes

Servings: 6

Ingredients:

- 4 sea bass fillets, skinless, each about 6 ounces

- Chicken rub as needed

- 8 tablespoons butter, unsalted

- 2 tablespoons chopped thyme leaves

- Lemon slices for serving

For the Marinade:

- 1 lemon, juiced

- 4 teaspoons minced garlic

- 1 tablespoon chopped thyme

- 1 teaspoon blackened rub

- 1 tablespoon chopped oregano

- 1/4 cup oil

Directions:

1.   Prepare the steep and for this, take a small dish, place all of its ingredients in it, stir until well pick up a small bowl, put all of its fixings in it, stir until well combined, and then pour the mixture dish, place all of its elements in it.

2.   Stir until well combined, and then pour the mixture into a large plastic bag.

3.	Add fillets in the bag, seal it, turn it upside down to coat fillets with the marinade and let it marinate for a minimum of 30 minutes in the refrigerator.

4.	When ready to cook, switch on the wood pellet grill, fill the grill hopper with apple-flavored wood pellets, power the grill on by using the control panel, press 'smoke' on the temperature dial, or set the temperature to 325 degrees F and let it preheat for a minimum of 15 minutes.

5.	Meanwhile, take a large baking pan and place butter on it.

6.	When the grill has preheated, open the lid, place baking pan on the grill grate, and wait until butter melts.

7.	Remove fillets from the marinade, pour marinade into the pan with melted butter, then season fillets with chicken rubs until coated on all sides, then place them into the pan, shut the grill and cook for 30 minutes until internal temperature reaches 160 degrees F, frequently basting with the butter sauce.

8.	When done, transfer fillets to a dish, sprinkle with thyme and then serve with lemon slices.

Sriracha Salmon

Preparation Time: 2 Hours and 10 Minutes

Cooking Time: 25 Minutes

Servings: 4

Ingredients:

- 3-pound salmon, skin on

For the Marinade:

- 1 teaspoon lime zest

- 1 tablespoon minced garlic

- 1 tablespoon grated ginger

- Sea salt as needed

- Ground black pepper as needed

- 1/4 cup maple syrup

- 2 tablespoons soy sauce

- 2 tablespoons Sriracha sauce

- 1 tablespoon toasted sesame oil

- 1 tablespoon rice vinegar

- 1 teaspoon toasted sesame seeds

Directions:

1.   Prepare the marinade and for this, take a small bowl, place all of its ingredients in it, stir until well combined, and then pour the mixture into a large plastic bag.

2.	Add salmon in the bag, seal it, turn it upside down to coat salmon with the marinade and let it marinate for a minimum of 2 hours in the refrigerator.

3.	When ready to cook, switch on the wood pellet grill, fill the grill hopper with flavored wood pellets, power the grill on then select 'smoke' on the temperature dial, or set the temperature to 450 degrees F.

4.	Let it preheat for a margin of 5 minutes.

5.	Meanwhile, take a large baking sheet, line it with parchment paper, place salmon on its skin-side down and then brush with the marinade.

6.	When the grill has preheated, open the lid, place baking sheet containing salmon on the grill grate, shut the grill and smoke for 25 minutes until thoroughly cooked.

7.	When done, transfer salmon to a dish and then serve.

Grilled Calamari

Preparation Time: 2 Hour

Cooking Time: 2 Hours

Servings: 6

Ingredients:

- 1 lb Calamari, cleaned

For the Brine:

- 1/4 cup salt

- 1 tablespoon ground black pepper

- 1/2 cup brown sugar

- 2 tablespoons soy sauce

Directions:

1.   Prepare the brine and for this, take a large container, add all of its ingredients in it, stir until sugar has dissolved, then add trout and let soak for 1 hour in the refrigerator.

2.   When ready to cook, switch on the wood pellet grill, fill the grill hopper with oak flavored wood pellets, power the grill on by using the control panel, pick 'smoke' on the temperature dial, or set the temperature to 205 degrees F and let it preheat for a minimum of 15 minutes.

3.   Meanwhile, remove trout from the brine and pat dry with paper towels.

4.   When the grill has preheated, open the lid, place trout on the grill grate, shut the grill and smoke for 2 hours until thoroughly cooked and tender.

5.   When done, transfer trout to a dish and then serve.

DELICIOUS MEAT RECIPES

Crown Rack of Lamb

Preparation Time: 30 Minutes | Cooking Time: 30 Minutes | Servings: 6

2 racks of lamb. Frenched
1 tbsp garlic, crushed
1 tbsp rosemary
1/2 cup olive oil
Kitchen twine

1. Preheat your Wood Pellet Grill to 450 0 F.
2. Rinse the lab with clean cold water then pat it dry with a paper towel.
3. Lay the lamb flat on a chopping board and score a ¼ inch down between the bones. Repeat the process between the bones on each lamb rack. Set aside.
4. In a small mixing bowl, combine garlic, rosemary, and oil. Brush the lamb of rack generously with the mixture.
5. Bend the lamb rack into a semicircle then place the frames together such that the bones will be up and will form a crown shape.
6. Wrap around 4 times starting from the base moving upward. Tie tightly to keep the racks together.
7. Place the lambs on a baking sheet and set in the Traeger. Cook on high heat for 10 minutes. Reduce the temperature to 300 0 F and cook for 20 more minutes or until the internal temperature reaches 130 0 F.
8. Remove the lamb rack from the Traeger and let rest while wrapped in a foil for 15 minutes.
9. Serve when hot.

Spicy Chunk Cheeseburgers

Prep time: 15 minutes | Cook time: 30 minute | Serves 4

1 lb (454 g) ground chuck (80% lean, 20% fat)
4 Monterey Jack cheese slices
¼ cup yellow onion, finely chopped
4 hamburger buns
2 tablespoon hatch chiles, peeled and chopped
6 tablespoon hatch chile salsa
1 teaspoon kosher salt
Mayonnaise, to taste
1 teaspoon ground black pepper

1. In a bowl, combine beef, diced onion, chopped hatch chiles, salt, and fresh ground pepper. Once evenly mixed, shape into 4 burger patties
2. Preheat pellet grill to 350°F (177°C)
3. Place burgers on grill, and cook for about 6 minutes per side or until both sides of each burger are slightly crispy
4. After burger is cooked to desired doneness and both sides have light sear, place cheese slices on each burger. Allow to heat for around 45 seconds or until cheese melts
5. Remove from grill and allow to rest for about 10 minute6. Spread a little bit of mayonnaise on both sides of each bun. Place burger patty on bottom side of the bun, then top with hatch chile salsa on top to taste

Grill a Burger Without Flipping Them

Preparation Time: 15 minutes | Cooking Time: 45-50 minutes | Servings: 6

1 Ground Beef Patties
Beef Rub
Cheese Pretzel buns

Start with cold but not frozen patties and sprinkle on the Beef Rub and massage into both side of the patty.
Preheat grill to 250 degrees and cook for 45 minutes
Add cheese and other topic varieties of your liking
Close the grill back up and let them finish for another 10 minutes before removing

Bacon-Swiss Cheesesteak Meatloaf

Preparation Time: 15 minutes | Cooking Time: 2 hours | Servings: 8-10

1 tablespoon canola oil
2 garlic cloves, finely chopped
1 medium onion, finely chopped
1 poblano chile, stemmed, seeded, and finely chopped
2 pounds extra-lean ground beef
2 tablespoons Montreal steak seasoning
1 tablespoon A.1. Steak Sauce
½ pound bacon, cooked and crumbled
2 cups shredded Swiss cheese
1 egg, beaten
2 cups breadcrumbs
½ cup Tiger Sauce

On your stove top, heat the canola oil in a medium sauté pan over medium-high heat. Add the garlic, onion, and poblano, and sauté for 3 to 5 minutes, or until the onion is just barely translucent.

Supply your smoker with wood pellets and follow the manufacturer's specific start-up procedure. Preheat, with the lid closed, to 225°F.

In a large bowl, combine the sautéed vegetables, ground beef, steak seasoning, steak sauce, bacon, Swiss cheese, egg, and breadcrumbs. Mix with your hands until well incorporated, then shape into a loaf.

Put the meatloaf in a cast iron skillet and place it on the grill. Insert meat thermometer inserted in the loaf reads 165°F.

Top with the meatloaf with the Tiger Sauce, remove from the grill, and let rest for about 10 minutes before serving.

London Broil

Preparation Time: 20 minutes | Cooking Time: 12-16 minutes | Servings: 3-4

1 (1½- to 2-pound) London broil or top round steak
¼ cup soy sauce
2 tablespoons white wine
2 tablespoons extra-virgin olive oil
¼ cup chopped scallions
2 tablespoons packed brown sugar
2 garlic cloves, minced
2 teaspoons red pepper flakes
1 teaspoon freshly ground black pepper

Using a meat mallet, pound the steak lightly all over on both sides to break down its fibers and tenderize. You are not trying to pound down the thickness.

In a medium bowl, make the marinade by combining the soy sauce, white wine, olive oil, scallions, brown sugar, garlic, red pepper flakes, and black pepper.

Put the steak in a shallow plastic container with a lid and pour the marinade over the meat. Cover and refrigerate for 4 hours.

Supply your smoker with wood pellets and follow the manufacturer's specific start-up procedure. Preheat, with the lid closed, to 350°F.

Place the steak directly on the grill, close the lid, and smoke for 6 minutes. Flip, then smoke with the lid closed for 6 to 10 minutes more, or until a meat thermometer inserted in the meat reads 130°F for medium-rare.

The meat's temperature will rise by about 5 degrees while it rests.

French Onion Burgers

Preparation Time: 35 minutes | Cooking Time: 20-25 minutes | Servings: 4

1-pound lean ground beef
1 tablespoon minced garlic
1 teaspoon Better Than Bouillon Beef Base
1 teaspoon dried chives
1 teaspoon freshly ground black pepper
8 slices Gruyère cheese, divided
½ cup soy sauce
1 tablespoon extra-virgin olive oil
1 teaspoon liquid smoke
3 medium onions, cut into thick slices (do not separate the rings)
1 loaf French bread, cut into 8 slices
4 slices provolone cheese

In a large bowl, mix together the ground beef, minced garlic, beef base, chives, and pepper until well blended.

Divide the meat mixture and shape into 8 thin burger patties.

Top each of 4 patties with one slice of Gruyère, then top with the remaining 4 patties to create 4 stuffed burgers.

Supply your smoker with wood pellets and follow the manufacturer's specific start-up procedure. Preheat, with the lid closed, to 425°F.

Arrange the burgers directly on one side of the grill, close the lid, and smoke for 10 minutes. Flip and smoke with the lid closed for 10 to 15 minutes more, or until a meat thermometer inserted in the burgers reads 160°F. Add another Gruyère slice to the burgers during the last 5 minutes of smoking to melt.

Meanwhile, in a small bowl, combine the soy sauce, olive oil, and liq uid smoke.

Arrange the onion slices on the grill and baste on both sides with the soy sauce mixture. Smoke with the lid closed for 20 minutes, flipping halfway through.

Lightly toast the French bread slices on the grill. Layer each of 4 slices with a burger patty, a slice of provolone cheese, and some of the smoked onions. Top each with another slice of toasted French bread. Serve immediately.

Beef Shoulder Clod

Preparation Time: 10 minutes | Cooking Time: 12-16 hours | Servings: 16-20

½ cup sea salt
½ cup freshly ground black pepper
1 tablespoon red pepper flakes
1 tablespoon minced garlic
1 tablespoon cayenne pepper
1 tablespoon smoked paprika 1 (13- to 15-pound) beef shoulder clod

Combine spices
Generously apply it to the beef shoulder.
Supply your smoker with wood pellets and follow the manufacturer's specific start-up procedure. Preheat, with the lid closed, to 250°F.
Put the meat on the grill grate, close the lid, and smoke for 12 to 16 hours, or until a meat thermometer inserted deeply into the beef reads 195°F. You may need to cover the clod with aluminum foil toward the end of smoking to prevent overbrowning. Let the meat rest and serve:

Corned Beef and Cabbage

Preparation Time: 30 minutes | Cooking Time: 4-5 hours | Servings: 6-8

:

1-gallon water

1 (3- to 4-pound) point cut corned beef brisket with pickling spice packet

1 tablespoon freshly ground black pepper

1 tablespoon garlic powder ½ cup molasses

1 teaspoon ground mustard

1 head green cabbage

4 tablespoons (½ stick) butter

2 tablespoons rendered bacon fat 1 chicken bouillon cube, crushed

Refrigerate overnight, changing the water as often as you remember to do so—ideally, every 3 hours while you're awake—to soak out some of the curing salt initially added.

Supply your smoker with wood pellets and follow the manufacturer's specific start-up procedure. Preheat, with the lid closed, to 275°F.

Remove the meat from the brining liquid, pat it dry, and generously rub with the black pepper and garlic powder.

Put the seasoned corned beef directly on the grill, fat-side up, close the lid, and grill for 2 hours. Remove from the grill when done.

In a small bowl, combine the molasses and ground mustard and pour half of this mixture into the bottom of a disposable aluminum pan.

Transfer the meat to the pan, fat-side up, and pour the remaining molasses mixture on top, spreading it evenly over the meat. Cover tightly with aluminum foil.

Transfer the pan to the grill, close the lid, and continue smoking the corned beef for 2 to 3 hours, or until a meat thermometer inserted in the thickest part reads 185°F.

Cheeseburger Hand Pies

Preparation Time: 35 minutes | Cooking Time: 10 minutes | Servings: 6

:

½ pound lean ground beef

1 tablespoon minced onion

1 tablespoon steak seasoning

1 cup cheese

8 slices white American cheese, divided

2 (14-ounce) refrigerated prepared pizza dough sheets, divided

2 eggs

24 hamburger dill pickle chips

2 tablespoons sesame seeds

6 slices tomato, for garnish Ketchup and mustard, for serving

Supply your smoker with wood pellets and follow the manufacturer's specific start-up procedure. Preheat, with the lid closed, to 325°F.

On your stove top, in a medium sauté pan over medium-high heat, brown the ground beef for 4 to 5 minutes, or until cooked through. Add the minced onion and steak seasoning.

Toss in the shredded cheese blend and 2 slices of American cheese and stir until melted and fully incorporated.

Remove the cheeseburger mixture from the heat and set aside.Make sure the dough is well chilled for easier handling. Working quickly, roll out one prepared pizza crust on parchment paper and brush with half of the egg wash.Arrange the remaining 6 slices of American cheese on the dough to outline 6 hand pies.

Pastrami

Preparation Time: 10 minutes | Cooking Time: 4-5 hours | Servings: 12

1-gallon water, plus ½ cup
½ cup packed light brown sugar
1 (3- to 4-pound) point cut corned beef brisket with brine mix packet
2 tablespoons freshly ground black pepper
¼ cup ground coriander

Cover and refrigerate overnight, changing the water as often as you remember to do so—ideally, every 3 hours while you're awake—to soak out some of the curing salt originally added.

Supply your smoker with wood pellets and follow the manufacturer's specific start-up procedure. Preheat, with the lid closed, to 275°F.

In a small bowl, combine the black pepper and ground coriander to form a rub.

Drain the meat, pat it dry, and generously coat on all sides with the rub.

Place the corned beef directly on the grill, fat-side up, close the lid, and smoke for 3 hours to 3 hours 30 minutes, or until a meat thermometer inserted in the thickest part reads 175°F to 185°F.

Add the corned beef, cover tightly with aluminum foil, and smoke on the grill with the lid closed for an additional 30 minutes to 1 hour.

Remove the meat

Refrigerate

Grilled Beef Jerky

Preparation Time: 15 minutes | Cooking Time: 5 hours | Servings: 10

3 pounds sirloin steaks
2 cups soy sauce
1 cup pineapple juice
1/2 cup brown sugar
2 tbsp sriracha
2 tbsp hoisin
2 tbsp red pepper flake
2 tbsp rice wine vinegar
2 tbsp onion powder

Mix the marinade in a zip lock bag and add the beef. Mix until well coated and remove as much air as possible.

Place the bag in a fridge and let marinate overnight or for 6 hours.

Remove the bag from the fridge an hour prior to cooking

Startup the Traeger and set it on the smoking settings or at 1900F.

Lay the meat on the grill leaving a half-inch space between the pieces. Let cool for 5 hours and turn after 2 hours.

Remove from the grill and let cool. Serve or refrigerate

Smoked Beef Roast

Preparation Time: 10 minutes | Cooking Time: 6 hours | Servings: 6

1-3/4 pounds beef sirloin tip roast
1/2 cup barbeque rub
2 bottles amber beer
1 bottle BBQ sauce

Turn the Traeger onto the smoke setting.

Rub the beef with barbeque rub until well coated then place on the grill. Let smoke for 4 hours while flipping every 1 hour.

Transfer the beef to a pan and add the beer. The beef should be 1/2 way covered.

Braise the beef until fork tender. It will take 3 hours on the stovetop and 60 minutes on the instant pot.

Remove the beef from the ban and reserve 1 cup of the cooking liquid.

Use 2 forks to shred the beef into small pieces then return to the pan with the reserved braising liquid. Add BBQ sauce and stir well then keep warm until serving. You can also reheat if it gets cold.

Reverse Seared Flank Steak

Preparation Time: 10 minutes | Cooking Time: 20 minutes | Servings: 2

:

3 pound flank steaks
1 tbsp salt
1/2 tbsp onion powder 1/4 tbsp garlic powder
1/2 black pepper, coarsely ground

Preheat the Traeger to 2250F.
Add the steaks and rub them generously with the rub mixture.
Place the steak
Let cook until its internal temperature is 100F under your desired temperature. 1150F for rare, 1250F for the medium rear and 1350F for medium.
Wrap the steak with foil and raise the grill temperature to high.
Place back the steak and grill for 3 minutes on each side.
Pat with butter and serve when hot.

Classic Texas Smoked Brisket

Prep time: 15 minutes | Cook time: 16 to 20 hours | Serves 12 to 15

1 (12-pound / 340-g) full packer brisket
2 tablespoons yellow mustard
1 batch espresso brisket rub
Worcestershire mop and spritz, for spritzing

1. Supply your Traeger with wood pellets and follow the start-up procedure. Preheat the grill, with the lid closed, to 225°F (107°C).
2. Using a boning knife, carefully remove all but about ½ inch of the large layer of fat covering one side of your brisket.
3. Coat the brisket all over with mustard and season it with the rub. Using your hands, work the rub into the meat. Pour the mop into a spray bottle.
4. Place the brisket directly on the grill grate and smoke until its internal temperature reaches 195°F (91°C), spritzing it every hour with the mop.
5. Pull the brisket from the grill and wrap it completely in aluminum foil or butcher paper. Place the wrapped brisket in a cooler, cover the cooler, and let it rest for 1 or 2 hours.
6. Remove the brisket from the cooler and unwrap it.
7. Separate the brisket point from the flat by cutting along the fat layer and slice the flat. The point can be saved for burnt ends (see Sweet Heat Burnt Ends), or sliced and served as well.

Homemade Mesquite Smoked Brisket

Prep time: 15 minutes | Cook time: 12 to 16 hours | Serves 8 to 12

1 (12-pound / 340-g) full packer brisket
2 tablespoons yellow mustard (you can also use soy sauce)
Salt, to taste
Freshly ground black pepper, to taste
1. Supply your Traeger with wood pellets and follow the start-up procedure. Preheat the grill, with the lid closed, to 225°F (107°C).
2. Using a boning knife, carefully remove all but about ½ inch of the large layer of fat covering one side of your brisket.
3. Coat the brisket all over with mustard and season it with salt and pepper.
4. Place the brisket directly on the grill grate and smoke until its internal temperature reaches 160°F (71°C) and the brisket has formed a dark bark.
5. Pull the brisket from the grill and wrap it completely in aluminum foil or butcher paper.
6. Increase the grill's temperature to 350°F (177°C) and return the wrapped brisket to it. Continue to cook until its internal temperature reaches 190°F (88°C).
7. Transfer the wrapped brisket to a cooler, cover the cooler, and let the brisket rest for 1 or 2 hours.
8. Remove the brisket from the cooler and unwrap it.
9. Separate the brisket point from the flat by cutting along the fat layer, and slice the flat. The point can be saved for burnt ends (see Sweet Heat Burnt Ends), or sliced and served as well.

Smoked Burnt Ends

Prep time: 30 minute | Cook time: 6 hours | Serves 8 to 10

1 (6-pound / 170-g) brisket point
2 tablespoons yellow mustard
1 batch sweet brown sugar rub
2 tablespoons honey
1 cup barbecue sauce
2 tablespoons light brown sugar

1. Supply your Traeger with wood pellets and follow the start-up procedure. Preheat the grill, with the lid closed, to 225°F (107°C).
2. Using a boning knife, carefully remove all but about ½ inch of the large layer of fat covering one side of your brisket point.
3. Coat the point all over with mustard and season it with the rub. Using your hands, work the rub into the meat.
4. Place the point directly on the grill grate and smoke until its internal temperature reaches 165°F (74°C).
5. Pull the brisket from the grill and wrap it completely in aluminum foil or butcher paper.
6. Increase the grill's temperature to 350°F (177°C) and return the wrapped brisket to it. Continue to cook until its internal temperature reaches 185°F (85°C).
7. Remove the point from the grill, unwrap it, and cut the meat into 1-inch cubes. Place the cubes in an aluminum pan and stir in the honey, barbecue sauce, and brown sugar.
8. Place the pan in the grill and smoke the beef cubes for 1 hour more, uncovered. Remove the burnt ends from the grill and serve immediately.

Reverse-Seared Tri-Tip Roast

Prep time: 10 minute | Cook time: 2 to 3 hours | Serves 4

1½ pounds (680 g) Tri-Tip roast
1 batch Espresso Brisket Rub
1. Supply your Traeger with wood pellets and follow the start-up procedure. Preheat the grill, with the lid closed, to 180°F (82°C).
2. Season the Tri-Tip roast with the rub. Using your hands, work the rub into the meat.
3. Place the roast directly on the grill grate and smoke until its internal temperature reaches 140°F (60°C).
4. Increase the grill's temperature to 450°F and continue to cook until the roast's internal temperature reaches 145°F (63°C). This same techniq ue can be done over an open flame or in a cast-iron skillet with some butter.
5. Remove the Tri-Tip roast from the grill and let it rest 10 to 15 minutes, before slicing and serving.

Smoked Tri-Tip Roast

Prep time: 25 minutes | Cook time: 5 hours | Serves 4

1½ pounds (680 g) Tri-Tip roast
Salt, to taste
Freshly ground black pepper, to taste
2 teaspoons garlic powder
2 teaspoons lemon pepper
½ cup apple juice

1. Supply your Traeger with wood pellets and follow the start-up procedure. Preheat the grill, with the lid closed, to 180°F (82°C).
2. Season the Tri-Tip roast with salt, pepper, garlic powder, and lemon pepper. Using your hands, work the seasoning into the meat.
3. Place the roast directly on the grill grate and smoke for 4 hours.
4. Pull the Tri-Tip from the grill and place it on enough aluminum foil to wrap it completely.
5. Increase the grill's temperature to 375°F (191°C).
6. Fold in three sides of the foil around the roast and add the apple juice. Fold in the last side, completely enclosing the Tri-Tip and liquid. Return the wrapped Tri-Tip to the grill and cook for 45 minutes more.
7. Remove the Tri-Tip roast from the grill and let it rest for 10 to 15 minutes, before unwrapping, slicing, and serving.

Santa Maria Tri-Tip Bottom Sirloin

Prep time: 15 minutes | Cook time: 45 minutes to 1 hour | Serves 4

2 teaspoons sea salt
2 teaspoons freshly ground black pepper
2 teaspoons onion powder 2 teaspoons garlic powder 2 teaspoons
dried oregano
1 teaspoon cayenne pepper
1 teaspoon ground sage
1 teaspoon finely chopped fresh rosemary
1 (1½- to 2-pound / 680- to 907-g) tri-tip bottom sirloin

1. Supply your Traeger with wood pellets and follow the start-up
procedure. Preheat the grill, with the lid closed, to 425°F (218°C).
2. In a small bowl, combine the salt, pepper, onion powder, garlic
powder, oregano, cayenne pepper, sage, and rosemary to create a
rub.
3. Season the meat all over with the rub and lay it directly on the
grill.
4. Close the lid and smoke for 45 minutes to 1 hour, or until a meat
thermometer inserted in the thickest part of the meat reads 120°F
(49°C) for rare, 130°F (54°C) for medium-rare, or 140°F (60°C) for
medium, keeping in mind that the meat will come up in
temperature by about another 5°F (-15°C) during the rest period.
5. Remove the tri-tip from the heat, tent with aluminum foil, and let
rest for 15 minutes before slicing against the grain

Mustard Pulled Beef

Prep time: 25 minutes | Cook time: 12 to 14 hours | Serves 5 to 8

1 (4-pound / 1.8-kg) top round roast
2 tablespoons yellow mustard
1 batch Espresso Brisket Rub
½ cup beef broth

1. Supply your Traeger with wood pellets and follow the start-up procedure. Preheat the grill, with the lid closed, to 225°F (107°C).
2. Coat the top round roast all over with mustard and season it with the rub. Using your hands, work the rub into the meat.
3. Place the roast directly on the grill grate and smoke until its internal temperature reaches 160°F (71°C) and a dark bark has formed.
4. Pull the roast from the grill and place it on enough aluminum foil to wrap it completely.
5. Increase the grill's temperature to 350°F (177°C).
6. Fold in three sides of the foil around the roast and add the beef broth. Fold in the last side, completely enclosing the roast and liquid. Return the wrapped roast to the grill and cook until its internal temperature reaches 195°F (91°C).
7. Pull the roast from the grill and place it in a cooler. Cover the cooler and let the roast rest for 1 or 2 hours.
8. Remove the roast from the cooler and unwrap it. Pull apart the beef using just your fingers. Serve immediately.

Smoked Top Round Roast Beef

Prep time: 10 minute | Cook time: 12 to 14 hours | Serves 5 to 8

1 (4-pound / 1.8-kg) top round roast
1 batch Espresso Brisket Rub
1 tablespoon butter

1. Supply your Traeger with wood pellets and follow the start-up procedure. Preheat the grill, with the lid closed, to 180°F (82°C).
2. Season the top round roast with the rub. Using your hands, work the rub into the meat.
3. Place the roast directly on the grill grate and smoke until its internal temperature reaches 140°F (60°C). Remove the roast from the grill.
4. Place a cast-iron skillet on the grill grate and increase the grill's temperature to 450°F (232°C). Place the roast in the skillet, add the butter, and cook until its internal temperature reaches 145°F (63°C), flipping once after about 3 minutes.
5. Remove the roast from the grill and let it rest for 10 to 15 minutes, before slicing and serving.

Smoked Mustard Beef Ribs

Prep time: 25 minutes | Cook time: 4 to 6 hours | Serves 4 to 8

2 (2- or 3-pound / 907- or 1360-g) racks beef ribs
2 tablespoons yellow mustard
1 batch sweet and spicy cinnamon rub

1. Supply your Traeger with wood pellets and follow the start-up procedure. Preheat the grill, with the lid closed, to 225°F (107°C).
2. Remove the membrane from the backside of the ribs. This can be done by cutting just through the membrane in an X pattern and working a paper towel between the membrane and the ribs to pull it off.
3. Coat the ribs all over with mustard and season them with the rub. Using your hands, work the rub into the meat.
4. Place the ribs directly on the grill grate and smoke until their internal temperature reaches between 190°F (88°C) and 200°F (93°C).
5. Remove the racks from the grill and cut them into individual ribs. Serve immediately.

Braised Beef Short Ribs

Prep time: 25 minutes | Cook time: 4 hours | Serves 2 to 4

4 beef short ribs
Salt, to taste
Freshly ground black pepper, to taste
½ cup beef broth

1. Supply your Traeger with wood pellets and follow the start-up procedure. Preheat the grill, with the lid closed, to 180°F (82°C).
2. Season the ribs on both sides with salt and pepper.
3. Place the ribs directly on the grill grate and smoke for 3 hours.
4. Pull the ribs from the grill and place them on enough aluminum foil to wrap them completely.
5. Increase the grill's temperature to 375°F (191°C).
6. Fold in three sides of the foil around the ribs and add the beef broth. Fold in the last side, completely enclosing the ribs and liquid. Return the wrapped ribs to the grill and cook for 45 minutes more. Remove the short ribs from the grill, unwrap them, and serve immediately.

Roasted Prime Rib

Prep time: 15 minutes | Cook time: 4 or 5 hours | Serves 8 to 12

1 (3-bone) rib roast
Salt, to taste
Freshly ground black pepper, to taste
1 garlic clove, minced

1. Supply your Traeger with wood pellets and follow the start-up procedure. Preheat the grill, with the lid closed, to 360°F (182°C).
2. Season the roast all over with salt and pepper and, using your hands, rub it all over with the minced garlic.
3. Place the roast directly on the grill grate and smoke for 4 or 5 hours, until its internal temperature reaches 145°F (63°C) for medium-rare.
4. Remove the roast from the grill and let it rest for 15 minutes, before slicing and serving.

Smoked Pastrami

Prep time: 15 minutes | Cook time: 12 to 16 hours | Serves 6 to 8

1 (8-pound / 3.6-kg) corned beef brisket
2 tablespoons yellow mustard
1 batch Espresso Brisket Rub
Worcestershire Mop and Spritz, for spritzing

1. Supply your Traeger with wood pellets and follow the start-up procedure. Preheat the grill, with the lid closed, to 225°F (107°C).
2. Coat the brisket all over with mustard and season it with the rub. Using your hands, work the rub into the meat. Pour the mop into a spray bottle.
3. Place the brisket directly on the grill grate and smoke until its internal temperature reaches 195°F (91°C), spritzing it every hour with the mop.
4. Pull the corned beef brisket from the grill and wrap it completely in aluminum foil or butcher paper. Place the wrapped brisket in a cooler, cover the cooler, and let it rest for 1 or 2 hours.
5. Remove the corned beef from the cooler and unwrap it. Slice the corned beef and serve.

New York Steaks

Prep time: 15 minutes | Cook time: 1 to 2 hours | Serves 4

4 (1-inch-thick) New York steaks
2 tablespoons olive oil
Salt, to taste
Freshly ground black pepper, to taste

1. Supply your Traeger with wood pellets and follow the start-up procedure. Preheat the grill, with the lid closed, to 180°F (82°C).
2. Rub the steaks all over with olive oil and season both sides with salt and pepper.
3. Place the steaks directly on the grill grate and smoke for 1 hour.
4. Increase the grill's temperature to 375°F (191°C) and continue to cook until the steaks' internal temperature reaches 145°F (63°C) for medium-rare.
5. Remove the steaks and let them rest 5 minutes, before slicing and serving.

Reverse-Seared Sirlion Steaks

Prep time: 15 minutes | Cook time: 1 or 2 hours | Serves 4

- 4 (4-ounce / 113-g) sirloin steaks
- 2 tablespoons olive oil
- Salt, to taste
- Freshly ground black pepper, to taste
- 4 tablespoons butter

1. Supply your wood pellet grill with wood pellets and follow the start-up procedure. Preheat the grill, with the lid closed, to 180°F (82°C).
2. Rub the steaks all over with olive oil and season both sides with salt and pepper.
3. Place the steaks directly on the grill grate and smoke until their internal temperature reaches 135°F (57°C). Remove the steaks from the grill.
4. Place a cast-iron skillet on the grill grate and increase the grill's temperature to 450°F (232°C).
5. Place the steaks in the skillet and top each with 1 tablespoon of butter. Cook the steaks until their internal temperature reaches 145°F (63°C), flipping once after 2 or 3 minutes. (I recommend reverse-searing over an open flame rather than in the cast-iron skillet, if your grill has that option.) Remove the steaks and serve immediately.

Asian Sirloin Skewers

Prep time: 10 minutes | Cook time: 1⅓ hours | Serves 6

- 1½ pounds (680 g) top sirloin steak
- 6 garlic cloves, minced
- 1 red onion
- ⅓ cup sugar
- ¾ cup soy sauce
- 1 tablespoon ground ginger
- ¼ cup sesame oil
- 3 tablespoon sesame seeds
- ¼ cup vegetable oil Bamboo skewers

1. Cut sirloin steak into cubes, about 1 inch.

2. Cut red onion into chunks similar in size to the sirloin steak cubes.

3. In a bowl, combine and whisk soy sauce, sesame oil, vegetable oil, minced garlic, sugar, ginger, and sesame seeds.

4. Add steak to sauce bowl and toss to coat until steak is covered in the sauce.

5. Marinate for at least 1 hour in a refrigerator (if you are in a rush it's ok to skip this part, but you'll sacrifice a little bit of flavor).

6. Preheat pellet grill to 350°F (177°C).

7. Thread marinated beef and red onion pieces onto bamboo skewers.

8. Grill the skewers, turning after about 4 minutes. Cook for 8 minutes total or until meat reaches your desired doneness.

Tomahawk Ribeye Steak

Prep time: 45 minutes | Cook time: 1 or 2 hours | Serves 4 to 6

- 1 (2½- to 3½-lbs / 1.1- to 1.6-kg) tomahawk ribeye steak
- 5 garlic cloves, minced
- 2 tablespoon kosher salt
- 1 bundle fresh thyme
- 2 tablespoon ground black pepper
- 8 ounces butter stick
- 1 tablespoon garlic powder
- ⅛ cup olive oil

1. Mix rub ingredients (salt, black pepper, and garlic powder) in a small bowl. Use this mixture to season all sides of the ribeye steak generously. You can also substitute your favorite steak seasoning. After applying seasoning, let the steak rest at room temperature for at least 30 minute.

2. While the steak rests, preheat your pellet grill to 450°F (232°C) to 500°F (260°C) for searing.

3. Sear the steak for 5 minutes on each side. Halfway through each side (so after 2½ minutes), rotate the steak 90° to form grill marks on the tomahawk.

4. After the tomahawk steak has seared for 5 minutes on each side (10 minute total), move the steak to a raised rack.

5. Adjust your pellet grill's temperature to 250°F (121°C) and turn up smoke setting if applicable. Leave the lid open for a moment to help allow some heat to escape.

6. Stick your probe meat thermometer into the very center of the cut to measure internal temperature.

7. Place butter stick, garlic cloves, olive oil, and thyme in the aluminum pan. Then place the aluminum pan under the steak to

catch drippings. After a few minutes, the steak drippings and ingredients will mix together

8. Baste the steak with the aluminum pan mixture every 10 minute until the tomahawk steak reaches your desired doneness

9. Once the steak reaches its desired doneness, remove from the grill and place on a cutting board or serving dish. The steak should rest for 10-15 minutes before cutting/serving.

Spicy Beef Tenderloin

Prep time: 25 minutes | Cook time: 1¼ hours | Serves 6

- 2½ pounds (1.1 kg) center cut beef tenderloin, trimmed and tied if uneven
- 2 tablespoon unsalted butter, room temperature
- 6 tablespoon peppercorns, mixed colors
- 1 tablespoon kosher salt
- 1 cup parsley, chopped
- Horseradish sauce, on the side
- 4 tablespoon Dijon mustard

1. Coarsely grind peppercorn mixture into a bowl. Add parsley, mustard, butter, and salt. Mix until thoroughly combined.

2. Rub spiced butter mixture generously and thoroughly on all sides of the tenderloin. Coat completely and roll tenderloin in bowl if necessary to soak up as much seasoning as possible.

3. Preheat pellet grill to 450°F (232°C).

4. Place tenderloin on an elevated rack (important) and roast. Use a probe meat thermometer to measure internal temperature. Cook until the center of the tenderloin reaches a temperature of 130°F (54°C). This typically takes 30-45 minutes but could be more or less depending on the size of your tenderloin.

5. Once tenderloin reaches desired doneness, remove from grill and allow to rest for at least 15 minutes.

6. Move tenderloin to a cutting board and slice. Try to catch as many juices as possible. Garnish with additional parsley.

Korean Short Ribs

Prep time: 15 minutes | Cook time: 8 hours | Serves 5

- 3 lbs (1.4kg) beef short ribs
- 2 tablespoon sugar
- ¾ cup water
- 1 tablespoon ground black pepper
- 3 tablespoon white vinegar
- 2 tablespoon sesame oil
- 3 tablespoon soy sauce
- 6 cloves garlic, minced
- ⅓ cup light brown sugar
- ½ yellow onion, finely chopped

1. Combine soy sauce, water, and vinegar in a bowl. Mix and whisk in brown sugar, white sugar, pepper, sesame oil, garlic, and onion. Whisk until the sugars have completely dissolved.

2. Pour marinade into large bowl or baking pan with high sides. Dunk the short ribs in the marinade, coating completely. Cover marinaded short ribs with plastic wrap and refrigerate for 6 to 12 hours.

3. Preheat pellet grill to 225°F (107°C).

4. Remove plastic wrap from ribs and pull ribs out of marinade. Shake off any excess marinade and dispose of the contents left in the bowl.

5. Place ribs on grill and cook for about 6-8 hours, until ribs reach an internal temperature of 203°F (95°C). Measure using a probe meat thermometer.

6. Once ribs reach temperature, remove from grill and allow to rest for about 20 minute. Slice, serve, and enjoy!

Swiss Cheese Beef Meatloaf

Prep time: 15 minutes | Cook time: 2 hours | Serves 4

- 1 tablespoon canola oil
- 2 garlic cloves, finely chopped
- 1 medium onion, finely chopped
- 1 poblano chile, stemmed, seeded, and finely chopped
- 2 pounds extra-lean ground beef
- 2 tablespoons Montreal steak seasoning
- 1 tablespoon A.1. steak sauce
- ½ pound bacon, cooked and crumbled
- 2 cups shredded Swiss cheese
- 1 egg, beaten
- 2 cups breadcrumbs
- ½ cup Tiger Sauce

1. On your stove top, heat the canola oil in a medium sauté pan over medium-high heat. Add the garlic, onion, and poblano, and sauté for 3 to 5 minutes, or until the onion is just barely translucent.

2. Supply your smoker with wood pellets and follow the manufacturer's specific start-up procedure. Preheat, with the lid closed, to 225°F (107°C).

3. In a large bowl, combine the sautéed vegetables, ground beef, steak seasoning, steak sauce, bacon, Swiss cheese, egg, and breadcrumbs. Mix with your hands until well incorporated, then shape into a loaf.

4. Put the meatloaf in a cast iron skillet and place it on the grill. Close the lid and smoke for 2 hours, or until a meat thermometer inserted in the loaf reads 165°F (74°C).

5. Top with the meatloaf with the Tiger Sauce, remove from the grill, and let rest for about 10 minute before serving.

Homemade London Broil

Prep time: 15 minutes | Cook time: 12 to 16 minutes | Serves 4

- 1 (1½- to 2-pound / 680- to 907-g) London broil or top round steak
- ¼ cup soy sauce
- 2 tablespoons white wine
- 2 tablespoons extra-virgin olive oil
- ¼ cup chopped scallions
- 2 tablespoons packed brown sugar
- 2 garlic cloves, minced
- 2 teaspoons red pepper flakes
- 1 teaspoon freshly ground black pepper

1. Using a meat mallet, pound the steak lightly all over on both sides to break down its fibers and tenderize. You are not trying to pound down the thickness.

2. In a medium bowl, make the marinade by combining the soy sauce, white wine, olive oil, scallions, brown sugar, garlic, red pepper flakes, and black pepper.

3. Put the steak in a shallow plastic container with a lid and pour the marinade over the meat. Cover and refrigerate for at least 4 hours.

4. Remove the steak from the marinade, shaking off any excess, and discard the marinade.

5. Supply your smoker with wood pellets and follow the manufacturer's specific start-up procedure. Preheat, with the lid closed, to 350°F (177°C).

6. Place the steak directly on the grill, close the lid, and smoke for 6 minutes. Flip, then smoke with the lid closed for 6 to 10 minute more, or until a meat thermometer inserted in the meat reads 130°F (54°C) for medium-rare.

7. Let the steak rest for about 10 minute before slicing and serving.
The meat's temperature will rise by about 5 degrees while it rests

Texas Beef Shoulder Clod

Prep time: 15 minutes | Cook time: 12 to 16 hours | Serves 16 to 20

- ½ cup sea salt
- ½ cup freshly ground black pepper
- 1 tablespoon red pepper flakes
- 1 tablespoon minced garlic
- 1 tablespoon cayenne pepper
- 1 tablespoon smoked paprika
- 1 (13- to 15-pound / 5.9- to 6.8-kg) beef shoulder clod

1. In a small bowl, combine the salt, pepper, red pepper flakes, minced garlic, cayenne pepper, and smoked paprika to create a rub. Generously apply it to the beef shoulder.

2. Supply your smoker with wood pellets and follow the manufacturer's specific start-up procedure. Preheat, with the lid closed, to 250°F (121°C).

3. Put the meat on the grill grate, close the lid, and smoke for 12 to 16 hours, or until a meat thermometer inserted deeply into the beef reads 195°F (91°C). You may need to cover the clod with aluminum foil toward the end of smoking to prevent overbrowning.

4. Let the meat rest for about 15 minutes before slicing against the grain and serving

Smoked Cheeseburger

Prep time: 35 minutes | Cook time: 10 minutes | Serves 4

- ½ pound lean ground beef
- 1 tablespoon minced onion
- 1 tablespoon steak seasoning
- 1 cup shredded Monterey Jack and Colby cheese blend
- 8 slices white American cheese, divided
- 2 (14-ounce / 397-g) refrigerated prepared pizza dough sheets, divided
- 2 eggs, beaten with 2 tablespoons water (egg wash), divided
- 24 hamburger dill pickle chips
- 2 tablespoons sesame seeds
- 6 slices tomato, for garnish
- Ketchup and mustard, for serving

1. Supply your smoker with wood pellets and follow the manufacturer's specific start-up procedure. Preheat, with the lid closed, to 325°F (163°C).

2. On your stove top, in a medium sauté pan over medium-high heat, brown the ground beef for 4 to 5 minutes, or until cooked through. Add the minced onion and steak seasoning.

3. Toss in the shredded cheese blend and 2 slices of American cheese, and stir until melted and fully incorporated.

4. Remove the cheeseburger mixture from the heat and set aside.

5. Make sure the dough is well chilled for easier handling. Working quickly, roll out one prepared pizza crust on parchment paper and brush with half of the egg wash.

6. Arrange the remaining 6 slices of American cheese on the dough to outline 6 hand pies.

7. Top each cheese slice with ¼ cup of the cheeseburger mixture, spreading slightly inside the imaginary lines of the hand pies.

8. Place 4 pickle slices on top of the filling for each pie.

9. Top the whole thing with the other prepared pizza crust and cut between the cheese slices to create 6 hand pies.

10. Using kitchen scissors, cut the parchment to further separate the pies, but leave them on the paper.

11. Using a fork dipped in egg wash, seal the edges of the pies on all sides. Baste the tops of the pies with the remaining egg wash and sprinkle with the sesame seeds.

12. Remove the pies from the parchment paper and gently place on the grill grate. Close the lid and smoke for 5 minutes, then carefully flip and smoke with the lid closed for 5 more minutes, or until browned.

13. Top with the sliced tomato and serve with ketchup and mustard.

Spiced Brisket

Prep time: 15 minutes | Cook time: 9 hours | Serves 8

Rub:
- 2 tablespoons onion powder
- 2 tablespoons garlic powder
- 2 teaspoons chile powder
- 2 tablespoons paprika
- ⅓ cup coarse ground black pepper
- ⅓ cup jacobsen salt or kosher salt

Brisket:
- 1 (12- to 14-pound / 5.4- to 6.4-kg) whole packer brisket, trimmed
- 1½ cup beef broth

1. In a small bowl, thoroughly combine all the rub ingredients. Season the brisket with the rub on all sides.
2. When ready to cook, set wood pellet grill temperature to 225°F (107°C) and preheat, lid closed for 15 minutes. For optimal flavor, use Super Smoke if available.
3. Place the brisket, fat-side down, on the grill and cook for about 5 to 6 hour, or until it reaches an internal temperature of 160°F (71°C).
4. Remove the brisket from the grill and wrap in a double layer of foil, then add the beef broth to the foil packet.
5. Return the foiled brisket to the grill and cook for about another 3 hours, or until it reaches an internal temperature of 204°F (96°C).
6. Remove the brisket from grill and unwrap from foil. Allow to rest for 15 minutes. Slice the brisket against the grain and serve warm.

Dijon Corned Beef Brisket

Prep time: 15 minutes | Cook time: 5 hours | Serves 4

- 1 (3-pound / 1.4-kg) flat cut corned beef brisket, fat cap at least ¼ inch thick
- ¼ cup Dijon mustard
- 1 bottle Traeger Apricot BBQ Sauce

1. Remove the brisket from its packaging and discard the spice packet, if any. Soak the brisket in water for at least 8 hours, changing the water every 2 hours.
2. When ready to cook, set wood pellet grill temperature to 275°F (135°C) and preheat, lid closed for 15 minutes.
3. Place the brisket, fat-side up, directly on the grill and cook for 2 hours.
4. Meanwhile, whisk the remaining ingredients together in a medium bowl. Pour half of the sauce mixture into the bottom of a disposable aluminum foil pan.
5. Using tongs, transfer the brisket, fat-side up, to the pan. Pour the remaining sauce mixture over the top of the brisket, spreading the sauce evenly with a spatula. Cover the pan tightly with aluminum foil.
6. Return the brisket to the grill and cook for an additional 2 to 3 hours, or until the brisket is tender and reaches an internal temperature of 203°F (95°C).
7. Let the brisket cool for 15 to 20 minutes. Slice the brisket across the grain and serve warm.

Smoked Wagyu Tri-Tip

Prep time: 5 minutes | Cook time: 1 hour | Serves 4

- 1 Wagyu beef tri-tip, trimmed
- ½ cup Traeger Prime Rib Rub

1. Generously season the tri-tip with Prime Rib Rub.
2. When ready to cook, set wood pellet grill temperature to 225°F (107°C) and preheat, lid closed for 15 minutes. For optimal flavor, use Super Smoke if available.
3. Put the tri-tip on the grill and cook for 1 to 1½ hours, or until it reaches an internal temperature of 130°F (54°C).
4. Remove the tri-tip from the grill and set aside.
5. Increase the grill temperature to 475°F (246°C). After 15 minutes, return the tri-tip to the grill and cook each side for 3 minutes.
6. Remove the tri-tip from the grill and slice to serve.

Brined Brisket

Prep time: 20 minutes | Cook time: 7 hours | Serves 4

- 1 cup brown sugar
- ½ cup kosher salt
- 1 (5- to 7-pound / 2.3- to 3.2-kg) flat cut brisket
- ¼ cup Traeger Beef Rub

1. Dissolve the sugar and salt in 6 quarts boiling water. Add 6 cups ice then let it cool. Put the brisket into the brine and cover. Place the brine in the refrigerator overnight.
2. Remove the brisket from the brine and pat dry with paper towels. Evenly sprinkle Beef Rub on the brisket.
3. When ready to cook, set wood pellet grill temperature to 250°F (121°C) and preheat, lid closed for 15 minutes.
4. Put the brisket, fat-cap down, on the grill and smoke for 3 hours.
5. Remove the brisket from the grill and wrap in a double layer of foil. Increase the grill temperature to 275°F (135°C) and cook for an additional 3 to 4 hours, or until the internal temperature reaches 204°F (96°C) on a meat thermometer.
6. Unwrap the brisket and place it on the grill and cook for 30 minutes more.
7. Remove the brisket from the grill and cool for 15 minutes before slicing against the grain and serving.

Garlic-Parmesan Crusted Filet Mignon

Prep time: 15 minutes | Cook time: 10 minutes | Serves 4

- 8 filet Mignon steaks
- 2 teaspoons garlic salt
- 2 teaspoons black pepper
- 2 teaspoons salt
- 2 cup grated Parmesan cheese
- 8 garlic, minced
- 2 tablespoons Dijon mustard

1. Season the filets with garlic salt, pepper, and salt. Combine the cheese and minced garlic in a shallow bowl.
2. When ready to cook, set wood pellet grill temperature to High and preheat, lid closed for 15 minutes.
3. Put the filets on the grill and cook each side for 4 minutes. When done, spread the Dijon mustard onto the filets, then dredge in the cheese-garlic mixture. Return the filets to the grill and cook for an additional 1 to 2 minutes, or until the cheese melts.
4. Cool for 5 minutes before serving.

Coffee Rub Brisket

Prep time: 15 minutes | Cook time: 9 hours | Serves 8

- 15 pounds (6.8 kg) whole packer brisket
- 1½ cups water, divided
- 2 tablespoons Traeger Coffee Rub, divided
- 2 tablespoons salt, divided

1. Trim the excess fat off the brisket, leaving a ¼-inch cap on the bottom.
2. In a small bowl, mix together 1 cup of water, 1 tablespoon of rub, and 1 tablespoon of salt. Keep stirring until most of the salt is dissolved.
3. Inject the brisket every square inch or so with the rub mixture. Season the exterior of the brisket with the remaining 1 tablespoon of rub and salt.
4. When ready to cook, set the wood pellet grill to 250°F (121°C) and preheat, lid closed for 15 minutes.
5. Put the brisket directly on the grill and cook until it reaches an internal temperature of 160°F (71°C), about 6 hours.
6. Wrap the brisket in two layers of foil and pour the remaining ½ cup of water into the foil packet. Secure tin foil tightly to contain the liquid. Increase the grill temperature to 275°F (135°C) and place the brisket back on the grill. Cook for another 3 hours, or until the internal temperature reaches 204°F (96°C).
7. Remove the brisket from the grill and slice to serve.

Porterhouse Steaks with Greens

Prep time: 10 minutes | Cook time: 1 hour 20 minutes | Serves 4

- 2 Porterhouse steaks
- Kosher salt and cracked black pepper, to taste
- 6 tablespoons butter, divided
- 1 shallot, thinly sliced
- 2 clove garlic, minced
- 1 cup heavy cream
- 1 pinch ground nutmeg
- 3 pounds (1.4 kg) mixed salad greens

1. Generously season the steaks with salt and pepper on both sides.

2. When ready to cook, set the wood pellet grill to 225°F (107°C) and preheat, lid closed for 15 minutes.

3. Put the seasoned steaks directly on the grill and cook until the internal temperature registers 120°F (49°C), for 45 minutes.

4. Remove the steaks from the grill and increase the temperature to 450°F (232°C). Let the grill preheat with the lid closed for 15 minutes.

5. Return the steaks to the hot grill and cook for an additional 5 to 6 minutes per side, or until the internal temperature reaches 130°F (54°C) for medium rare. Remove the steaks from the grill and set aside to cool.

6. For the creamed greens: Heat 2 tablespoons of the butter in a saucepan over high heat until it foams. Add the shallot and garlic and cook over medium-low heat for about 5 minutes, stirring often, or until softened.

7. Stir in the heavy cream and bring to a simmer. Cook for about 10 minutes until slightly thickened. Sprinkle with the nutmeg and season with salt to taste. Purée the ingredients with a hand blender until smooth. Set aside.

8. Heat the remaining 4 tablespoons of butter in a large pot over high heat until it foams. Add the greens and cook for about 5 minutes, stirring constantly, or until they are tender but still bright green.

9. Season as needed with salt and add the cream mixture. Reduce the heat, cover, and allow to simmer for 5 minutes more until cooked through.

10. To serve, slice the steaks and serve on top of the creamed greens.

Bacon-Onion Jam Strip Steaks

Prep time: 10 minutes | Cook time: 1 hour | Serves 2

- 2 whole New York strip steaks, room temperature
- Traeger Prime Rib Rub, to taste
- ½ pound (227 g) bacon, cut into small pieces
- 1 small sweet onion
- ¼ cup brown sugar
- ¼ cup apple juice
- 3 tablespoons strong brewed coffee
- ½ tablespoon balsamic vinegar
- Extra-virgin olive oil, as needed

1. Season the steaks with Prime Rib Rub on both sides. Set aside.
2. When ready to cook, start the wood pellet grill to 350°F (177°C) and preheat, lid closed for 15 minutes.
3. Put the bacon pieces in a cast iron pan and place on the hot grill. Cook for 10 to 15 minutes until the fat is rendered.
4. Remove the bacon from the pan and drain out all but 1 tablespoon of the bacon grease from the pan.
5. Add the onion to the cast iron pan and cook for about 10 minutes on the grill, or until the onion is tender. Add the brown sugar and cook for about another 15 to 20 minutes, or until the onion begins to caramelize.
6. Stir in the apple juice, coffee, and cooked bacon and continue to cook for about 20 minutes, stirring occasionally.
7. Pour in the balsamic vinegar and spoon into a bowl and set aside.
8. Turn the heat on the Traeger to High and allow to preheat for 15 minutes with the lid closed.
9. Lightly drizzle the olive oil over the steaks and place them on the grill. Cook each side for about 4 to 5 minutes, for medium-rare, or until cooked to your desired doneness.

10. Remove the steaks from the grill and cool for about 10 minutes before slicing. Serve the steaks topped with the bacon-onion jam.

Texas Smoked Brisket

Prep time: 15 minutes | Cook time: 10 hours | Serves 8

- 1 (14- to 18-pound / 6.4- to 8.2-kg) whole packer brisket, trimmed
- Meat Church Holy Cow BBQ Rub
- Meat Church Holy Gospel BBQ Rub

1. Season the brisket with Meat Church Holy Cow Rub on all sides. Optionally add a light layer of Meat Church Holy Gospel Rub. Allow the brisket to sit for 20 to 30 minutes.

2. When ready to cook, set the wood pellet grill temperature to 275°F (135°C) and preheat, lid closed for 15 minutes.

3. Put the brisket, fat side up, on the grill and cook for about 5 to 6 hours, or until it reaches an internal temperature of 165°F (74°C).

4. Remove the brisket from the grill and wrap tightly in Traeger Butcher Paper.

5. Return the wrapped brisket to the grill and continue to cook for about 3 to 4 hours, or until it reaches an internal temperature of 204°F (96°C).

6. Remove the brisket from the grill and rest for 30 minutes. Unwrap the brisket and slice against the grain before serving.

Bacon-Wrapped Tenderloin

Prep time: 10 minutes | Cook time: 1 hour | Serves 4

- 4 pounds (1.8 kg) beef tenderloin
- 4 ounces (113 g) Traeger Beef Rub
- 4 ounces (113 g) Traeger Coffee Rub
- 8 strips bacon

1. When ready to cook, set the wood pellet grill to 275°F (135°C) and preheat, lid closed for 15 minutes.
2. Lightly season the beef tenderloin with the beef rub and wrap with the bacon. Season again with another layer of coffee rub.
3. Put the tenderloin directly on the grill and cook for 30 minutes, or until it reaches an internal temperature of 120°F (49°C). If not, continue to cook, checking every 5 minutes until cooked to the desired temperature.
4. Remove the tenderloin from the grill and increase the temperature to 450°F (232°C).
5. After 10 minutes, place the tenderloin back on the grill and sear for 5 minutes, or until it reaches a finished internal temperature of 135°F (57°C). If not, flip the tenderloin and cook for another 5 minutes.
6. Remove the tenderloin from the grill and cool for 10 minutes before slicing and serving.

Buttered Smoked Porterhouse Steak

Prep time: 15 minutes | Cook time: 45 minutes | Serves 2

- 4 tablespoons butter, melted
- 2 teaspoons Dijon mustard
- 2 tablespoons Worcestershire sauce
- 40 ounces (1.1 kg) Porterhouse steaks
- 1 teaspoon Traeger Coffee Rub

1. When ready to cook, set the wood pellet grill to 180°F (82°C) and preheat, lid closed for 15 minutes. For optimal flavor, use Super Smoke if available.

2. Whisk the melted butter, mustard, and Worcestershire sauce together in a small bowl until smooth. Brush the mixture on both sides of the steaks. Season both sides of the steaks with Traeger Coffee Rub.

3. Place the steaks directly on the grill and smoke for 30 minutes. With tongs, transfer the steaks to a plate.

4. Increase the grill temperature to High and preheat. For optimal results, set to 500°F (260°C) if available. Brush the steaks again with the butter mixture.

5. Place the steaks back on the grill and continue to cook until the desired internal temperature is reached, 130°F (54°C) for medium rare, 135°F (57°C) for medium-well.

6. Cool for 5 minutes before serving.

Marinated London Broil with Butter Cheese

Prep time: 10 minutes | Cook time: 1 hour 20 minutes | Serves 4

Marinade:
- ¼ cup water
- ¼ cup soy sauce
- 1 clove garlic, minced
- 1 small onion, coarsely chopped
- 2 tablespoons vegetable oil or extra-virgin olive oil
- 2 tablespoons red wine vinegar
- 1 tablespoon ketchup
- 1 teaspoon sugar
- 1 teaspoon Worcestershire sauce
- 1 teaspoon freshly ground black pepper

Steak:
- 1 (2-pound / 907-g) top round London broil steak
- Traeger Beef Rub, as needed Butter Cheese:
- 8 tablespoons butter, softened
- ¼ cup crumbled blue cheese
- 1 teaspoon Worcestershire sauce
- 1 scallion, minced
- Freshly ground black pepper, to taste

1. Whisk all the marinade ingredients to combine in a small bowl.

2. Put the steak into a large resealable plastic bag and pour in the marinade. Let sit in the refrigerator for 6 hours to overnight.

3. Remove the steak from the refrigerator and rest to room temperature.

4. In a separate bowl, combine all the ingredients for the butter cheese and stir to mix well. Cover and refrigerate, if not using immediately.

5. When steak is at room temperature, discard the marinade and pat dry with paper towels, then season with Traeger Beef Rub on all sides.

6. When ready to cook, set the wood pellet grill temperature to 180°F (82°C) and preheat, lid closed for 15 minutes.

7. Arrange the steak directly on the grill and smoke for 60 minutes. With tongs, transfer the steak to a platter.

8. Increase the temperature to 500°F (260°C) and preheat with the lid closed for 10 to 15 minutes.

9. Place the steak back on the grill and cook for about 15 to 20 minutes, or until the desired internal temperature is reached, 130°F (54°C) for medium-rare.

10. Let the steak rest for 5 minutes before thinly slicing on a diagonal. Serve the steak alongside the prepared butter cheese.

Grilled Bloody Mary Flank Steak

Prep time: 8 hours | Cook time: 15 minutes | Serves 4

1½ pounds (680 g) flank steak

Marinade:
- 2 cup Traeger Smoked Bloody Mary Mix
- ½ cup vodka
- ½ cup vegetable oil
- 3 clove garlic, minced
- 1 whole lemon or lime, juiced
- 1 tablespoon Worcestershire sauce
- 1 teaspoon celery salt
- 1 teaspoon coarse ground black pepper
- Hot sauce, to taste

1. Whisk together all the ingredients except the steak in a small bowl until combined.

2. Place the steak in a resealable plastic bag and pour half the marinade over it. Allow to marinate for at least 6 hours or overnight. Refrigerate the remaining half of the marinade in an airtight container.

3. When ready to cook, set the wood pellet grill temperature to High and preheat.

4. Pour the remaining marinade into a small saucepan and let simmer over medium heat until it has reduced by half. Keep warm and set aside.

5. Drain the steak and discard the marinade. Pat it dry with paper towels.

6. Arrange the steak directly on the grill and cook each side for 7 to 10 minutes.

7. Transfer the steak to a cutting board and cool for 3 minutes before thinly slicing on a sharp diagonal.

Smoked Tomahawk Steak

Prep time: 5 minutes | Cook time: 1 hour | Serves 4

- 1 (32-ounce / 907-g) bone-in Tomahawk rib-eye steak, 2 inch thick
- Kosher salt, to taste
- Meat Church Holy Cow BBQ Rub
- 3 tablespoons butter

1. Lightly season the steak on all sides with salt. Let sit at room temperature for 1 hour.
2. When ready to cook, set wood pellet grill temperature to 225°F (107°C) and preheat, lid closed for 15 minutes. For optimal flavor, use Super Smoke if available.
3. Rinse the steak and pat it dry with paper towels. Liberally season both sides of the steak with Meat Church Holy Cow BBQ Rub.
4. Arrange the steak directly on the grill and cook for about 45 minutes, or until it reaches an internal temperature of 120°F (49°C). The cooking time depends on the thickness.
5. Remove the steak from the grill and rest for 10 minutes lightly tented with aluminum foil.
6. Meanwhile, put a cast iron skillet on the grill. Increase the grill temperature to 500°F (260°C).
7. Put the steak on the dry cast iron griddle and sear for 1 minute. Flip the steak and sear for 1 minute more. Doing this should bring your steak to an internal temperature of no more than 130°F (54°C).
8. Remove the steak and top with a generous amount of butter. Continue to cook for about 5 minutes, or until the internal temperature registers 130°F (54°C), for medium-rare.
9. Let the steak rest for 10 minutes before slicing and serving.

Cocoa-Rubbed Steak for Two

Prep time: 50 minutes | Cook time: 50 minutes | Serves 4

- 2 whole rib-eye roast, trimmed
- 1 cup Traeger Coffee Rub¼ cup cocoa powder

1. Cut the roast into 2½-inch-thick steaks. Reserve 2 steaks and freeze the remaining steaks for later use.
2. Mix the Traeger Coffee rub and cocoa powder in a bowl. Season the steaks lightly with the rub mixture. Reserve the remaining rub mixture for later use. Allow the steaks to sit at room temperature for 45 minutes.
3. When ready to cook, set the wood pellet grill to 225°F (107°C) and preheat, lid closed for 15 minutes.
4. Lay the steaks on the hot grill and cook for 40 minutes, flipping the steaks halfway through, or until the desired internal temperature is reached, between 105 to 110°F (41 to 43°C).
5. Remove the steaks from the grill and allow to rest on the counter.
6. Increase the temperature to High and preheat, lid closed for 15 minutes. For optimal results, set to 500°F (260°C) if available.
7. Return the steaks to the grill and cook for 8 minutes, flipping the steaks halfway through the cooking time, or until it reaches a finished temperature of 130°F (54°C), for medium rare.
8. Cool for 5 minutes before serving.

TEXAS
BARBECUE

- THE -
EST. OLD 1999
TEXAS
PITMASTER
TRAVIS COUNTY

- THE -
EST. OLD 1999
TEXAS
PITMASTER
TRAVIS COUNTY